CHOCTAW

CHOCTAW
A CULTURAL AWAKENING

PHOTOGRAPHY BY DAVID G. FITZGERALD

TEXT BY MEMBERS AND EMPLOYEES OF THE CHOCTAW NATION

COMPILED BY JUDY ALLEN

CHOCTAW NATION PRESS

*For Rainette Rowland,
my photographic assistant, and a tribal member
of the Choctaw Nation of Oklahoma.*

—David G. Fitzgerald

◆

▲ Shoulder sash. Courtesy of the National Museum of the American Indian, Cultural Resources Center, (18439.000).

◀ Page 1: This black pottery bowl, circa 1830, is from the Kate McClendon Collection. Courtesy of the Oklahoma History Center and the Oklahoma Historical Society.

Photographs © 2012 by David G. Fitzgerald
Text © 2012 by Judy Allen except for the following:

"An Indigenous Choctaw History" and "Arrows: Beautifully Engineered Weapons" © 2012 by Dr. Ian Thompson

"A Brief History of the Choctaw Nation and Wheelock" © 2012 by Louis Coleman

"A Brief History of Choctaw Hymns" © 2012 by Virginia Espinoza

"Choctaw Church Convention" © 2012 by Eleanor Caldwell

"Lighthorsemen of Choctaw Nation Upheld the Law" © 2012 by Bill Coleman Sr.

"The Final Choctaw Dawes Commission Rolls" © 2012 by Brenda S. Hampton

All rights reserved. No part of this book may be reproduced or transmitted in any form or by any means, electronic or mechanical including photocopying, recording, or by any information storage and retrieval systems without written permission from the Choctaw Nation of Oklahoma except by a reviewer who may quote brief passages in review.

Library of Congress Control Number: 2012949042
EAN: 978-0-615-66205-3

Published by Choctaw Nation Press
PO Box 1210
Durant OK 74702
580-924-8280

Project Manager: Douglas A. Pfeiffer
Jacket and book design: Elizabeth Watson
Editor: Kathy Howard

Printed and bound in the United States of America
Printed by Texoma Print Services
10 9 8 7 6 5 4 3 2 1

Front cover photo: Choctaw Nation Chief Gregory E. Pyle and Assistant Chief Gary Batton pictured at the Tribal Capitol building on the Tvshka Homma grounds. "It is vital that heritage and culture are passed down to each generation to ensure the longevity of our future as a tribal people," said Chief Pyle. "Choctaws have much to be proud of, yet it is my hope that our descendants have even greater self-sufficiency, health, and success than their forefathers."
Back cover photo: Pictured at the Oklahoma State Capitol are Choctaw Nation Head Start students from the center in Coalgate. The children were featured performers of Choctaw Social Dances at the Capitol. Pictured with the rotunda in the background are (back row) Kale Horton, Rylie Blue, Caleb Hopkins, and (front) Bentley Hill, Damian Martinez, Jett Burris, and Nekota Wainscott.

ACKNOWLEDGMENTS

This book is dedicated to Choctaw people everywhere. *Choctaw: A Cultural Awakening* has been a work of passion for many Choctaw people. The entire tribal public relations team has assisted in coordinating the efforts to produce ideas, material, and photographs for this book.

On the "wish list" for several years, this book finally became a real project when renowned photographer David Fitzgerald was contracted to provide his talent for the project. Rainette Rowland, his gifted assistant, is a member of the Choctaw Nation of Oklahoma, and her enthusiasm and enjoyment for each and every photo has helped make this work a pleasurable experience. David and Rainette's collaboration is largely responsible for the true beauty of this book.

A special word of appreciation goes to Lana Sleeper and Janine Dills for the many calls they placed to assist in research and scheduling. I owe a tremendous thanks to Lisa Reed for her support, talent, and assistance from day one. Lisa not only has great ideas for photo opportunities, but she has been willing to research details as a follow-up for the many pictures.

The School of Choctaw Language has been very helpful in this endeavor and all of the projects the Public Relations Department works on. A very sincere thank you to all the teachers and staff in the Language Department. Thanks are due to the Historic Preservation Department and Director Ian Thompson for his many hours of dedication, and also to Tribal Membership Director Melissa Jones for her help. Others who deserve special acknowledgment include Sue Folsom, Vonna Shults, Melissa Stevens, Lorene Blaine, and many, many others who helped in coordinating details to make this book possible.

I appreciate everyone who participated in the photography sessions and the many data checks, and also all the people who answered a seemingly infinite number of questions. Thank you very much.

I also must express gratitude to my family, especially my husband, Ray, for patiently allowing time for me to put in long hours at my computer to work on this book on behalf of the Choctaw Nation.

Team members Doug Pfeiffer, Kathy Howard, and Betty Watson have led me through the maze of the publishing world with professional courtesy and shared their vast experience of book production so that a spectacular Choctaw book can be on our shelves. Doug helped the Choctaw Nation print shop, Texoma Print Services, managed by Russell Marcum, physically publish the book. Kathy edited the text (mine and all of the other Choctaw tribal members who submitted pieces for the book), and Betty worked magic with the layout of the photos and all the content. Their advice and wisdom are greatly appreciated. Thank you to all of them.

Most of all, I would like to acknowledge the support of Chief Gregory E. Pyle, Assistant Chief Gary Batton, and the Tribal Council. The tribal leadership's focus on tribal heritage and their vision toward the future have made the cultural awakening of the Choctaw Nation a reality. —Judy Allen

This book is dedicated to Choctaw people everywhere.

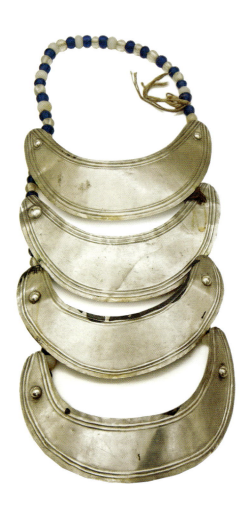

▲ Mississippi Choctaw breastplate collected in 1908. Courtesy of the National Museum of the American Indian, Cultural Resources Center, (109078.000).

CONTENTS

ACKNOWLEDGMENTS 5   INTRODUCTION: OUR HERITAGE JOURNEY 11

1 Remember Our Paths 15
WALKING THE TALK: SERVANT LEADERSHIP
An Indigenous Choctaw History 19

2 A Cultural Awakening 29
REVITALIZING CHOCTAW HERITAGE
A Brief History of the Choctaw Nation and Wheelock 31

3 Foundation of Faith 57
BUILT ON THE SOLID ROCK
Choctaw Church Convention 59

4 Beauty in Many Forms 70
CELEBRATING ART AND CULTURE

5 Chahta Warrior Pride 101
TVSHKA HOMMA

Lighthorsemen of the Choctaw Nation Upheld the Law 103

6 Tribal Services and Systems 127
ENDURING SINCE THE FOUNDATION OF OUR GOVERNMENT

The Final Choctaw Dawes Commission Rolls 129

7 A Taste Of Choctaw 145
SHARING THE SAVOR

8 Choctaw People from All Walks of Life 157
GROWING WITH PRIDE, HOPE, AND SUCCESS

BIBLIOGRAPHY FOR AN INDIGENOUS CHOCTAW HISTORY 196

INDEX 198

101

127

157

145

▶ OVERLEAF: CHOCTAW SOCIAL DANCES ARE AN IMPORTANT PART OF FESTIVALS AND CEREMONIES. THE DANCES ARE A WAY TO KEEP CHOCTAW HERITAGE ALIVE.

INTRODUCTION

◆

Our Heritage Journey

CHOCTAW: *A CULTURAL AWAKENING* is a celebration of the revival of heritage the descendants of the Trail of Tears are experiencing. Dr. Ian Thompson, the Director of the Choctaw Nation Historic Preservation Department, begins this book with details of the Choctaw origin legend, through the years it has taken to bring the tribal people from the ancestral homelands to what is now Oklahoma, to become the modern Native American families we see today.

After the deaths of so many tribal members resulting from the forced march along the Trail of Tears, the Choctaws concentrated much of their efforts for the next 150 years on education, faith, homes, and food for friends and family. As their ancestors had done for centuries, the Choctaw adapted their way of life to survive. Art and dance were not always seen as vital skills to be passed on through the generations. Out of necessity, time was spent on learning survival expertise. Crops were planted and harvested. Boys were taught to hunt and fish. Girls learned to gather natural herbs, berries, and nuts and to cook and make clothing. Families who managed to keep the Choctaw language and heritage alive during those decades are now helping teach others.

Integration with people of European culture and the Christian missionaries had a tremendous influence upon Choctaw ancestors. New customs were soon accepted by the tribal members. Government schools offered education to the young people. Speaking in the English language was encouraged while speaking in the Choctaw language was strongly discouraged. Wheelock Academy was one of the first schools established in the Choctaw Nation, as told in the Cultural Awakening section by historian Louis Coleman.

The photographs of Skullyville Cemetery show that some of the earliest burials after the Trail of Tears were in marked gravesites. Others were placed in plots that remain unmarked today. The Historic Preservation Department of the Choctaw Nation sometimes uses ground-penetrating radar equipment in an attempt to identify those graves, as seen in the Tribal Services and Systems section featuring the photo of Assistant Chief Batton searching for the exact location of his great-grandfather's burial.

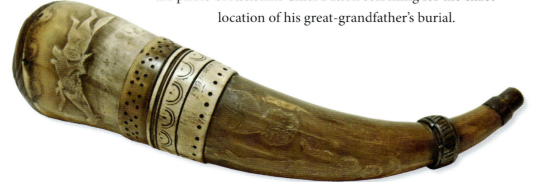

▲ CHOCTAW SHOULDER SASH WITH BELL, COLLECTED 1908. COURTESY OF THE NATIONAL MUSEUM OF THE AMERICAN INDIAN CULTURAL RESOURCES CENTER, (018857.000).

◀ CHOCTAW CALLING HORN, CIRCA 1861. DON J. FOLSOM COLLECTION. COURTESY OF THE OKLAHOMA HISTORY CENTER AND THE OKLAHOMA HISTORICAL SOCIETY, (02236).

◀◀ PRESLEY BYINGTON IN FULL REGALIA AT A CHOCTAW NATION–SPONSORED POW WOW.

CHOCTAW: A CULTURAL AWAKENING

The very design of the Great Seal of the Choctaw Nation epitomizes the warrior mind-set of the Choctaw men.

▶ THE CHOCTAW NATION TRIBAL COUNCIL: FROM LEFT TO RIGHT TED DOSH, KENNY BRYANT, PERRY THOMPSON, JAMES FRAZIER, TONY MESSENGER, RON PERRY, THOMAS WILLISTON, AND JOE COLEY AND SEATED FROM LEFT TO RIGHT, JACK AUSTIN, BOB PATE, ANTHONY DILLARD, AND DELTON COX.

Faith in the Creator has helped many a Choctaw family through troublesome times. The commentaries by Virginia Espinoza and Eleanor Caldwell will help bring readers up-to-date on how Choctaws have continued to worship God.

The very design of the Great Seal of the Choctaw Nation epitomizes the warrior mind-set of the Choctaw men. The seal is made up of three arrows representing the three historic warrior Chiefs: Pushmataha, Apukshunubbee, and Mushulatubbee; with a smoking pipe hatchet that was passed between Council members in times of both peace and war. The seal also features a bow made of sturdy bois d'arc, unstrung in times of peace, yet ready to be pulled taut at a moment's notice to protect the Tribe and family. Prior to statehood, this philosophy was

INTRODUCTION: OUR HERITAGE JOURNEY

The seal is made up of three arrows representing the three historic warrior Chiefs: Pushmataha, Apukshunubbee, and Mushulatubbee.

understood by a special breed of peacekeepers called Lighthorsemen—as explained in a narrative by Bill Coleman.

Beginning in 1899, the Dawes Commission parceled the land to individual ownership and assigned roll numbers to Indian people. Brenda Hampton, after working for the Tribe for twenty-six years in the Certificate of Degree of Indian Blood (CDIB)/Tribal Membership Department, had the expertise to explain the Dawes process. In order to be a member of the Tribe today, you have to trace lineal ancestry back to a Dawes Roll number.

The Chief and the Council have been learning and sharing art, dance, stickball, and the Choctaw language. They hope that as you enjoy this book, you truly do get a "taste" of Choctaw and even try some actual recipes! The leaders also hope everyone will gain tremendous pride in the people and the success of the Tribe the photos represent—the youth, the elders, and all who are in between. Wake up to Choctaw culture! Pass it on!

▼ STICKBALL SETS. COURTESY OF THE NATIONAL MUSEUM OF THE AMERICAN INDIAN CULTURAL RESOURCES CENTER, (018849.000, 018847.000, AND 018833.000).

1

REMEMBER OUR PATHS

WALKING THE TALK: SERVANT LEADERSHIP

The Choctaw Nation has grown both in membership and services in recent years. There are now more than 200,000 Choctaws worldwide, making this the third-largest Tribe in the United States.

The Miko (Chief) and Miko Apelvchi (Assistant Chief) believe in servant leadership. Both have been employees of the Tribe for many years, and have stepped into the role of leaders after decades of experience. Each has worked in different programs of the Choctaw Nation, and understands the importance of meeting the needs of tribal citizens.

Chief Gregory E. Pyle and Assistant Chief Gary Batton have been honored in Oklahoma and across the nation. They have stated one of their greatest marks of distinction was when the Tribe received the United States Freedom Award for the support shown to the employees in the National Guard and Reserves.

Economic development has expanded under the guidance of Chief Pyle and Assistant Chief Batton. They and the twelve members of the Tribal Council, through visionary initiatives, have launched successful business ventures on behalf of the Choctaw Nation. Thanks to this success, revenue can be reinvested into additional industry, jobs, and services for citizens and communities. These services include educational opportunities, youth programs, and elder centers.

The Tribal Council currently serving the Choctaw people are Thomas Williston, District 1; Tony Messenger, District 2; Kenny Bryant, District 3; Delton Cox, District 4; Ron Perry, District 5; Joe Coley, District 6; Jack Austin, District 7; Perry Thompson, District 8; Ted Dosh, District 9; Anthony Dillard, District 10; Bob Pate, District 11; and James Frazier, District 12.

The leaders of the Tribe have been at the forefront of the cultural awakening that tribal members have been experiencing. Requests for information on history, language, moccasin making, pottery, basketry, and weaponry are among the topics that have been shared through classes, *BISKINIK,* and other media in the past few years. The Chief, Assistant Chief, and Council have all supported the Historic Preservation Department, the Cultural Services Department, and all other tribal programs in efforts and events to share heritage information.

▲ Assistant Chief Gary Batton
◀ Chief Gregory E. Pyle

CHOCTAW: A CULTURAL AWAKENING

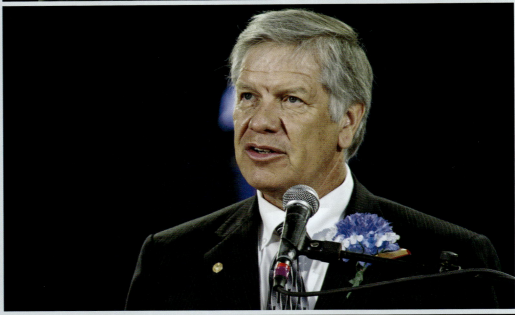

▲ On stage at the 2011 Labor Day festivities: (clockwise from top left) Storyteller Tim Tingle; Assistant Chief Gary Batton as master of ceremonies; Chief Gregory E. Pyle giving the State of the Nation address; Reverend Bertram Bobb replacing his hat after opening prayer; Sarah DeHerrera singing the National Anthem in Choctaw; and Speaker of Tribal Council Delton Cox.

REMEMBER OUR PATHS

▲▲ Chief Gregory E. Pyle with his hand on the Holy Bible held by his wife, Patti, as the oath of office is administered by Judge Mitch Mullin.

▲ Council members are sworn into office by Judge Fred Bobb at 2011 ceremonies. Pictured raising their hands and accepting responsibility as Tribal Council members are Thomas Williston, Ron Perry, Bob Pate, Perry Thompson, Kenny Bryant, and Tony Messenger.

An Indigenous Choctaw History

IAN THOMPSON, PHD

THREE HUNDRED YEARS AGO, Choctaw boys would begin their day by assembling early in the morning to learn from a respected elder man. He would teach them Choctaw values, life lessons, and history. Often, he would prefix a story with the words: *"Makato, makato, makato, achi-li"* (It was said and said and said, and I say), meaning that the oral history that he was about to relate had been handed down from generation to generation through time. Early Choctaw people honored ancestors, recognizing them as the progenitors of Choctaw family, community, and traditional knowledge. They passed down oral history because they knew that by enriching their lives with the lived experience of those who have come before, they were empowered to perceive things that lay beyond one lifetime's finite scope of vision. The lives of those who came before have no less relevance in the twenty-first century. While history is an important learning tool, the Choctaw ancestors also directly touched the present by sending prayers forward for their descendants who are living today and by passing on to today's Choctaw people the gifts of a living culture, language, and identity.

Early Choctaw history is a story of both people and the land. The Choctaw Nation of Oklahoma is a removed Tribe, forcefully separated from its original homeland

◀ A SMALL ROADSIDE AREA NEAR PHILADELPHIA, MISSISSIPPI, IS THE SITE OF THIS MARKER NOTING THE LOCATION OF THE SIGNING OF THE DANCING RABBIT CREEK TREATY OF 1830. THE CHOCTAWS WERE THE FIRST TO WALK THE TRAIL OF TEARS, ARRIVING IN INDIAN TERRITORY IN 1831.
▲ NANIH WAIYA MOUND.

CHOCTAW: A CULTURAL AWAKENING

▲ Cave of the creation legend.

Nanih Waiya … is both the most sacred spot on the Choctaw Homeland and the beginning point of Choctaw history.

Bowl made from hand-dug Oklahoma clay, sand, and burned shell, wood fired. By Dan Bernier, Choctaw traditional potter, woodworker, moccasin maker, and pottery instructor.

generations ago. Yet, this homeland is inseparable from early Choctaw history, and it continues to be part of Choctaw language and traditional culture for people living in Oklahoma and beyond. The geographic core of the original Choctaw homeland is located in what is today east-central Mississippi and western Alabama. This is where Choctaw towns were located before the Trail of Tears. However, farther back in time, groups ancestral to today's Choctaw people lived within a broader area that encompasses the southern two-thirds of Mississippi, much of western Alabama, northern Florida, and some parts of Louisiana. These ancestors lived their lives as a part of this land, and as a group, they had a connection with every stream, landform, and significant spot within it. As centuries have passed, the ancestors have literally become a physical part of the earth of the Choctaw homeland and of the plants and animals living there. If you spend time on this sacred land and clear your mind of the rush of today's life, you may hear their hushed voices blowing through the pine trees, sense their presence in the close canebrakes, and possibly catch a glinting spark as one returns to visit a familiar place on a dark night.

Nanih Waiya, located in what is today Winston County, Mississippi, is both the most sacred spot on the Choctaw homeland and the beginning point of Choctaw history. The Nanih Waiya area includes an ancient village and a nearby cave, which is located in the base of a hill. The name "Nanih Waiya" itself has different meanings in the Choctaw language, depending on slight differences in pronunciation. Some Choctaws call it "Nvnih Waiya," which means "sloping hill," a reference to a large earth mound located in the village. To others, it is "Nan Awaya," meaning "place where things grow," as Choctaw oral histories indicate that Nanih Waiya is where Choctaws began as a people.

Two basic origin traditions involving Nanih Waiya are told in Choctaw communities today; the same two basic stories were common in the 1720s, when they were first put into writing (e.g., Du Pratz 1758:326). According to one set of these accounts (e.g., Pistonatubbee, cited in Halbert 1899:229–230) the Choctaw were created underground, and emerged to the surface of the earth at Nanih Waiya Cave. Some of these earth emergence stories connect the creation of the Choctaw with that of other Tribes or even different insects. According to the other body of traditional Choctaw origin accounts (e.g., Peter Folsom, cited in Halbert 1899:228–229), the Choctaw migrated into the homeland. One common migration tradition indicates that the Choctaw and Chickasaw were formerly members of the same Tribe. Life became difficult, and a group led by a pair of brothers, Chahta and Chicasa, decided to emigrate. Each evening, a holy man stuck a sacred pole upright in the ground. Before morning, God would influence the pole to make the top of it lean in the direction that the people were to travel. Every morning for many months (years according to some accounts), it pointed toward the east. Finally, at Nanih Waiya, the pole remained upright all night and the people stopped. Chicasa took his followers (who became the Chickasaw people) to an area farther north; Chahta and his followers stayed and became the Choctaw people. Although different, these two basic groups of Choctaw origin stories do not necessarily contradict. Through time, a number of once-separate communities have joined the Choctaw Tribe. It is possible that the two stories relate to the origins of two of them. Both accounts make it clear that Nanih Waiya village was the first Choctaw settlement. It is where God handed down the basic parts of Choctaw society, including the iksa, or moiety, system that governed Choctaw social relations.

Today, Nanih Waiya Cave remains much as it has been for centuries. Years of plowing have severely damaged the Nanih Waiya village site. The most visible remnant is a pyramidal earth mound, measuring about twenty-five feet tall and covering nearly an acre at its base. To some Choctaws, this is the "Mother Mound." Created by ancestors one basket load of dirt at a time, some see this monumental architecture as a representation of the earth, the mother from which life physically originates. In Native Southeastern communities, the houses of village leaders, temples, and council houses were often erected on top of such earth mounds. At one time, there were two other earth mounds at Nanih Waiya (Choctaw tradition), along with a mile-and-a-half-long defensive wall made up of eighteen segments that surrounded the settlement, and two broad roads leading from the village to the north and southeast (Halbert 1899). The earliest visible traces at the village date back roughly 2,000 years, but Choctaw ancestors may have been at the site much earlier.

Several Choctaw oral traditions are set at the time of or shortly after the genesis of the Choctaw people at Nanih Waiya. Some of these stories describe a world that is different from today's. They attribute the formation of the Black Belt Prairie of western Alabama and northeastern Mississippi to herds of a type of giant animal that destroyed the bark and lower branches of the trees, killing them. According to the accounts, these animals went extinct quite some time ago (Claiborne 1880, 484).

Archaeology, the science of learning about past people by studying the things they left behind in the ground, contributes another dimension to Choctaw oral histories. A century of archaeological work has shown that people were living in the Choctaw homeland by at least 13,000 years ago during the end of the last Ice Age, and possibly earlier. Mirroring the Choctaw oral stories, archaeology has demonstrated that these

▲ A Choctaw doll, circa 1890, from Kate McClendon's Collection. Courtesy of the Oklahoma History Center and Oklahoma Historical Society, (02694).

CHOCTAW: A CULTURAL AWAKENING

Mirroring the Choctaw oral stories, archaeology has demonstrated that these people did indeed live side by side with species that have been extinct for more than 10,000 years.

▲ A Choctaw doll, circa 1890, from Kate McClendon's Collection. Courtesy of the Oklahoma History Center and Oklahoma Historical Society, (02692).

people did indeed live side by side with giant animals, such as the mastodon (a species of elephant), glyptodon (a giant armadillo-like animal), and the short-faced bear (eleven feet tall), that have been extinct for more than 10,000 years. Evidence suggests that the early people who lived with them were organized as small, mobile groups, which sometimes traveled great distances by foot. They made their living by gathering edible plants, and by hunting animals, even some of the giant ones (Martin and Klein 1984), using a type of throwing spear known as the atlatl.

The ancestors of today's Choctaw people were a dynamic, creative, flexible group. Their adaptability repeatedly helped them to overcome adversity and survive in an uncertain world. The last Ice Age ended approximately 12,000 years ago. With this climate change and the extinction of the large animals, people in the Choctaw homeland had to adapt their way of life to survive. They decreased their range of movement, focusing their activities within particular river drainages, specializing in hunting the white-tailed deer (Bushnell 1909:30) and gathering nuts (Morse et al 1996).

From 9500 BC until about 4000 BC, the climate continued to change, slowly becoming much like it is today. This had effects on the landscape: modern pine forest spread through much of the Southeast (Webb et al. 1993); sea level reached its present height; and the flow of streams slowed down (Schuldenrein 1996:26-27). These changes made local streams excellent habitat for edible freshwater mussels. As people began to rely on these localized food sources, they made more permanent settlements (Anderson and Sassaman 2004:95), as well as a number of cultural developments. Communities began to erect earth mounds as early as 5200 BC in northern Louisiana (Gibson and Shenkel 1988:9). Artisans developed a new technology for making tools and jewelry from ground stone. Items like baskets, bags, nets, cloth garments, earth ovens, wooden tools, boats, bone pins, needles, and awls seem to have become a lot more common (e.g., Purdy 1992). People to the north of the Choctaw homeland began to domesticate native plant foods, such as the gourd by 3000 BC, sunflower by 2800 BC, marsh elder by 1900 BC, and chenopod by 1700 BC (Smith 2006). Pottery was developed as early as 2500 BC on the Atlantic Coast of Georgia and South Carolina and by about 1000 BC it was common in the Choctaw homeland.

The prosperous communities within the Choctaw homeland grew significantly between the period of 1000 BC and AD 1000. Many villages were built on the Tombigbee and other local rivers (e.g., Jenkins and Kraus 1986). Two important developments during this period would change life there forever. One was the widespread adoption of the bow and arrow, around AD 700, which replaced the atlatl. Some Choctaw oral traditions depict the bow as a gift from God (Claiborne 1880:519). The second development was the widespread adoption of corn agriculture around AD 1000. Corn is the main ingredient for many of today's traditional Choctaw foods such as banaha and tanchi labona. According to one Choctaw oral tradition (Halbert 1899:231, also see Wright 1828:182), the Choctaw people obtained corn when a crow brought a single kernel north across the Gulf of Mexico to a Choctaw boy. Archaeology has since independently confirmed that corn agriculture did, in fact, originate in Mesoamerica, across the Gulf of Mexico from the Choctaw homeland (Mangelsdorf et al. 1964).

It appears that around AD 1000 many people moved out of the core area of the Choctaw homeland, and into neighboring regions that have large streams and excellent soil for growing corn. The abundance of food that the farmers provided here allowed some of these settlements to become very large. The biggest of these is today known

▲ Chief Gregory E. Pyle, Assistant Chief Gary Batton, and Executive Director of Public Relations Judy Allen look at the original Treaty of Dancing Rabbit Creek at the National Archives in Washington, D.C.

CHOCTAW: A CULTURAL AWAKENING

◀ Dr. Ian Thompson and wife, Amy, have helped revive the art of traditional pottery in the Choctaw Nation. They are teaching the step-by-step process, from digging and cleaning clay to the final phases of firing the pots.

▼ Moundville-style cooking pot in process of being fired.

Bowl made from hand-dug Oklahoma clay and sand, wood fired. By Theresa Prough, Choctaw traditional potter, moccasin maker, beadworker, and pottery instructor.

as Moundville. A recognized World Heritage Site, Moundville is located on the Black Warrior River, in Tuscaloosa County, Alabama. It is the second-largest precolonial construction north of Mexico, contiguously occupying seventy-five hectares, and including at least twenty-nine earth mounds (one as tall as a six-story building). By around AD 1250 the settlement and surrounding area incorporated perhaps 10,000 people (Knight and Steponaitis 1998:20). Moundville's occupants were the ancestors of today's Choctaw, as well as other local Tribes. During this period, other major ancestral Choctaw populations were living on the Tombigbee in western Alabama, in the area to the north of Nanih Waiya in east central Mississippi, on the Mobile River in southwestern Alabama, and on the Pearl River of south-central Mississippi (Carleton 1994; Galloway 1995:354; Livingood 2010).

For well over 10,000 years, the communities in and around the Choctaw homeland had a great deal of sovereignty in governing their own affairs and determining their own course of development. They were vibrant, prosperous, and strong. About twelve generations after Moundville reached its height, the ancestors of the Choctaw and other local Tribes found themselves violently swept into turbulent worldwide developments, with the arrival of European colonial powers in the Americas. As a whole, the Native American population, spanning North and South America, is believed to been larger than the population of Europe at the time of contact. However, European arrival precipitated the most horrific population crash in human history with as many as 95 percent of the Native people perishing. The sovereignty of the weakened Native American communities was severely challenged, along with their very existence. A number of them were destroyed; the survivors found ways to adapt.

Like many Native groups, the first significant contact that ancestral Choctaw people had with Europe involved its diseases more than its people. These were brought to the region by Spanish soldiers who shipwrecked on the Gulf Coast in the 1520s, and soon took the lives of half of the people living in some communities (Cabeza de Vaca 1905:34-35, 64 [1542]). Other equally deadly epidemics followed.

For some Choctaw ancestors, the first face-to-face contact with Europeans came in October 1540, when a group of Spanish conquistadors, lead by Hernando De Soto, came into the lands of the Mabilla, a Tribe that is ancestral to today's Choctaw people. De Soto's charter (Clayton et. al. 1993:359–364), handed down from the Spanish Crown, was to conquer, pacify, and populate lands through which he traveled. De Soto came to Atahachi, the town where the chief Tuscaloosa was residing, and proceeded to place him in chains and demand slave labor and women from him (Rangel 1993: 291 [ca.1540]). Tuscaloosa told De Soto that these things would be provided at the town of Mabila, if De Soto would accompany him there. Along the journey, the conquistadors pillaged local settlements (292). When one of the conquistadors disappeared while seeking to recapture a woman who had managed to escape him (Elvas 1993:98 [1557]), De Soto threatened to burn Tuscaloosa alive (Biedma 1993:233 [1544]). After the group entered Mabila, Tuscaloosa walked away from the conquistadors and rejoined his constituents. An angry Spaniard reacted by slashing a Native man in the back with a sword, killing him (Elvas 1993:99 [1557]). Upon this, the town's occupants drove the Spaniards outside of the walls, freeing the Native people whom the Spanish had taken as their slaves along their journey, and capturing nearly all of De Soto's army's supplies.

Although the Native warriors were superior to the Spanish foot soldiers (cf. Garcilaso 1993:259 [1596]), they were no match for the cavalry (Hudson 1976:113).

Like many Native groups, the first significant contact that ancestral Choctaw people had with Europe involved its diseases more than its people.

▲ A CHOCTAW DOLL, CIRCA 1890, FROM KATE MCCLENDON'S COLLECTION. COURTESY OF THE OKLAHOMA HISTORY CENTER AND OKLAHOMA HISTORICAL SOCIETY, (02695).

Over the course of many hours, the Spanish, behind their cavalry, counterattacked. The warriors repeatedly turned them back, inflicting heavy casualties, but eventually the conquistadors succeeded in reentering the town, setting it on fire, and killing all of the occupants. These Choctaw ancestors lost the battle and their lives that day, but they also gained an enduring victory. The conquistadors' original intent had been to conquer the land, take its resources, and subjugate its population (Clayton et. al. 1993:359-364). After seeing the bravery and love for freedom that these ancestral Choctaws possessed, the impressed conquistadors marveled that

> it was impossible to rule such bellicose people or to subjugate such bold men . . . it seemed to them that neither by force nor by persuasion could they be brought under the authority and dominion of the Spaniards; they [the Choctaw] would allow themselves to be killed first (Garcilaso 1993:356 [1596]).

For the next century, few Europeans entered the Choctaw homeland. Native communities reorganized. The De Soto chronicles mention a people known as the "Pafalaya" (an ancient tribal name for the Choctaw). However, it was not until 1675 that the name "Choctaw" itself first appeared in a European document. This document describes the Tribe as a large and powerful group with 107 villages, (Calderon 1675, cited in Galloway 1995:170). Clearly, these strong Choctaw communities had reorganized and regrouped from the losses suffered through battle and European diseases. One of their recovery strategies was to incorporate refugees from shattered neighboring communities. The Choctaw are known to have taken in survivors from the Chatot, Ibitoupa, Choula, Mobile, Okelousa, Pensacola, and Tohome Tribes (Swanton 1946:107, 108, 140, 151, 167, 173, 197).

French entrepreneurs permanently settled in Choctaw country in 1699, and cultivated an alliance with the Choctaw people. Many married into the Choctaw Tribe, and started French/Choctaw families. The two nations were trading partners through the French period (1699–1763). The neighboring Chickasaw and Creek Tribes allied with England, France's colonial rival. The English encouraged the Chickasaw and Creek to attack Choctaw communities to obtain Choctaw women and children to sell as slaves in the American Colonies. By 1700, these raids had resulted in 1,800 Choctaw men, women, and children killed, 500 women and children taken as slaves, and 800 Chickasaw warriors killed (Iberville 1981:172 [1702]). Within a few decades, loyalties within the Choctaw Tribe itself became divided between the French and English. The division brewed into the Choctaw Civil War of 1747–1750 (Pesantubbee 2005:38–45,50–53), in which several hundred Choctaw people lost their lives. A wave of European diseases hit simultaneously claiming even more Choctaw lives than the war did (Adair 1775:331).

When the American Revolutionary War began, some Choctaw warriors fought for the American Colonies (Dancing Rabbit Creek Treaty Article 21); others fought on the side of England in skirmishes against Spanish forces. Official relations with the United States began in 1786 with the signing of the Treaty of Hopewell (DeRosier 1970: 20). The Choctaw came to be strong allies of the United States, in 1801 giving up a portion of the sacred homeland in the Treaty of Fort Adams to help the fledgling nation buffer itself against a possible Napoleonic invasion from New Orleans (Green 1978:7). Choctaw warriors distinguished themselves fighting for the United States in the Creek War of 1813, and helped Andrew Jackson's forces save New Orleans, by then a US possession, from British invasion (DeRosier 1970:34-37).

▲ A Choctaw doll, circa 1890, from Kate McClendon's Collection. Courtesy of the Oklahoma History Center and Oklahoma Historical Society, (02688).

Although Jesuits had worked among the Choctaws during the French period with little success, in 1818, the American Board of Commissioners for Foreign Missions, with the support of Chiefs Pushmataha and Mushulatubbee began setting up Protestant missions and schools within Choctaw country (Kidwell 2008:203). Many Choctaws were eager for their children to attend the schools in hopes of learning the American way of thinking so that they could help the Tribe deal with the United States on more equal footing. Through these schools and missions, a number of Choctaw people were converted to the Methodist, Baptist, and Presbyterian faiths; some lifelong friendships developed, and Choctaws and missionaries worked together to put the Choctaw language into a system of writing that is still used today.

Through the early 1800s, Choctaw borders became increasingly crowded with illegal immigrants from the United States, many of whom were covetous of Choctaw-owned land. To satisfy their demands, the US government set up a system whereby Choctaw people were allowed to rack up debts to US trading companies (Perdue 1988:144). The government then demanded that these debts be paid off in the form of lands given up by treaty to the United States. Through a series of seven treaties, signed between 1801 and 1830, the Choctaw Tribe ceded all of the homeland, approximately 23,000,000 acres, to the United States in exchange for lands in what is now southeastern Oklahoma. Most Choctaw people opposed these agreements, and many obtained the right, through treaty, to become US citizens and stay in their homeland on personal allotments. Nevertheless, through fraud, home burning, and unprovoked attacks, most Choctaws, many of whom had risked their lives fighting to protect the United States just a few years earlier, were forced to emigrate to the lands the Tribe had received in the west.

The Choctaw journey to what is now Oklahoma was called the "Trail of Tears." The Choctaw Trail of Tears began with three exoduses during the winters of 1831 to 1833 in which about 12,000 Choctaw people removed from the homeland of their ancestors to present-day Oklahoma. Traveling parties took various routes on the 550-mile journey, but the two main branches of the Choctaw Trail of Tears led through Memphis, Tennessee, and Vicksburg, Mississippi, respectively. Along the way, conditions were often harsh, due to bad weather, mismanagement, and expense cutting on the part of the government. In some of the traveling parties, young and old people alike had to wade through miles of frigid, waist-high water, endure winter storms in open camps with no shelter and little clothing, and eat shortened rations of spoiled food. It is estimated that between 1,800 and 4,000 Choctaw people died from exposure, fatigue, disease, and murder on the Trail of Tears, while the US government turned a net profit of $3,000,000 (DeRosier 1970:163).

Several thousand Choctaws stayed in the homeland through the First Removal, but most were landless and faced continued fraud, persecution, and deadly abuse from American citizens (Tolbert 1975:66–67). A Second Choctaw Removal to what is now Oklahoma spanned from 1845 to 1854, and involved about 6,000 people. In the Third Choctaw Removal from 1902 to 1903, an additional 1,500 people emigrated to Oklahoma. Eventually, only about 1,000 Choctaw remained behind in Mississippi, forming the basis for today's Mississippi Band of Choctaw Indians. Once in Oklahoma, survivors of the Choctaw Trail of Tears drew upon a profound inner strength and optimism to rebuild their lives and families. On June 3, 1834, they formed the government of the Choctaw Nation (Baird 1973:49), and began a meteoric recovery that continues to this day.

Once in Oklahoma, survivors of the Choctaw Trail of Tears drew upon a profound inner strength and optimism to rebuild their lives and families. On June 3, 1834, they formed the government of the Choctaw Nation (Baird 1973:49), and began a meteoric recovery that continues to this day.

Bottle made from hand-dug Alabama clay and burned mussel shell, wood fired. By Vangie Robinson, Choctaw traditional potter and pottery instructor.

2

A Cultural Awakening

REVITALIZING CHOCTAW HERITAGE

A cultural awakening is being experienced today from coast to coast. Choctaw language classes are accredited at public schools across the Choctaw Nation as well as at several colleges and universities. Lessons are broadcast on the Internet and held in community centers, free of charge, by teachers who have been certified by the School of Choctaw Language.

Culture is being shared on a regular basis. Choctaw social dances are taught to students at all fourteen Head Start Centers and a dance troupe has been formed by employees of the Choctaw Nation. The first Monday of each month is Heritage Monday at tribal facilities, where traditional dress is encouraged and staff members are asked to share their heritage with visitors through language, history, and other innovative ways.

With an increased desire to learn about their customs, the Choctaw Nation is more proactive in sharing information with members. One of the unique opportunities for cultural education is the festival at the Smithsonian's National Museum of the American Indian (NMAI). The Choctaw Nation of Oklahoma was the first Indian Nation to host a tribal festival at NMAI, beginning this event in 2011. The Tribe also hosts the Labor Day gathering each year at the Capitol Grounds at Tvshka Homma, which centers around the museum, village activities, sports, music, and other events.

▲ This calling horn, circa 1916, is from the Helen Folsom Collection. Courtesy of the Oklahoma History Center and the Oklahoma Historical Society, (08136).

◄ A Commemorative Trail of Tears Walk is held annually to honor Choctaw ancestors and to celebrate the lives of their descendants. The custom of the official memorial walk began in 1992 when tribal members walked twenty-two miles from Horatio, Arkansas, to Eagletown, Oklahoma.

A Brief History of the Choctaw Nation and Wheelock

LOUIS COLEMAN

From time immemorial the Choctaws occupied a sizable portion of what would later become the southeastern United States. As one of the so-called Five Civilized Tribes, the Choctaws were a non-nomadic, peaceful group that practiced subsistence-type agriculture.

With the end of the War of 1812, a surge of settlers moved westward from the original British colonies into the continental interior. Under relentless pressure from the US government, the Choctaws ceded major portions of their national territory until, by the early 1800s, they were occupying only the central and southeastern portions of what would become the state of Mississippi in 1817. The influx of white settlers into the newly created state triggered a clash of cultures, a problem of dual sovereignty that boded ill for the Choctaws.

Choctaw leaders were well aware of the threat to tribal survival as an ethnic, self-governed entity. To deal with this threat, they sought help in the form of Christian missionaries who first came among them in 1818. The primary purpose of this action was to obtain education for tribal children. The missionaries established schools but encountered difficulty in their educational efforts because few Choctaws spoke English, and the missionary teachers could not speak Choctaw. To address this problem, the missionaries developed a written Choctaw language, creating the tools of that tongue.

The Choctaws, although essentially monotheistic, did not respond readily to the proselytizing efforts of the missionaries. But after almost a decade of such endeavors, the Choctaws began to adopt the new faith, possibly as a tactic in their struggle for independence and retention of their lands. Choctaw leaders nourished the hope that their adoption of American culture, religion, and education might allow them the freedom and independence they desired. Their hopes went unrealized, however, in the face of the constant pressure from the US and state governments to vacate their ancestral lands and move west of the Mississippi River.

Most of the Choctaws were adamantly opposed to the move but their leaders were realists who had become convinced that their only hope lay in moving away from the influence and pressure being applied to the Tribe. Finally, in 1830 the Choctaws signed a treaty with the US government, ceding their remaining Mississippi lands and agreeing to move to what would later become southeastern Oklahoma.

In 1830 the Choctaws signed a treaty with the US government, ceding their remaining Mississippi lands and agreeing to move to what would later become southeastern Oklahoma.

◄ Choctaw dancers on the plaza in front of the National Museum of the American Indian.
► Choctaw dancers on the capitol lawn.

▲ Alumni of Wheelock Academy often talk about both the good and sad memories they have of their lives at the school. Pushmataha Hall is pictured behind this group of alumni.

▶ The bell from Pushmataha Hall was sent to the original foundry for refurbishment in 2008. The inscription reads "DEFEND THE POOR AND FATHERLESS."

The Trail of Tears

THE CHOCTAWS ENDURED much suffering and many deaths on the extremely difficult trip to the new land. This led to the designation of the trek as the "Trail of Tears."

Neither the US government nor the Choctaws were prepared for the task of moving thousands of people several hundred miles over primitive roads and challenging terrain to the new land.

The US government had no experience in such an undertaking, the Choctaws being the first major Tribe to be moved. The logistics of such a project were especially difficult and often mismanaged. Adverse weather conditions during the move, such as heavy rains, snow, and freezing temperatures, were prevalent.

Before leaving Mississippi, the Choctaws numbered about 20,000. Of these, about 15,000 elected to move. These were divided into groups of several hundred to be escorted by federal officers and employees. An estimated 10 percent of the Choctaws perished on the trail and approximately 12,500 arrived in the new land between 1831 and 1833.

Many of the missionaries who had served the Choctaws in Mississippi were invited to join them in the new land and many did so, including the Rev. Alfred Wright and his wife, who were delayed several months on the trail because of his serious health problems. They arrived at the chosen site for their Wheelock Mission in mid-October, 1832.

Expansion of Wheelock and the Choctaw Educational System

WITH THE NEIGHBORHOOD schools in operation, there was a realization that for various reasons the education efforts were still not reaching many children. The Wrights expanded their station to board students who were not otherwise being served. The Wrights added to the mission homes to accommodate these students. Initially coeducational, Rev. Wright found problems with this situation and elected to limit the enrollment to girls. Thus the Wheelock Female Seminary came into being in the early 1840s.

In 1842 the Choctaw General Council enacted legislation creating a national education system to consist of a day and boarding schools to serve both boys and girls. Since the Wheelock Seminary was already in operation, it was incorporated into the national system, with the Choctaws sharing the cost of operation. The mission support group financed construction of the additional buildings needed. The Wheelock Seminary functioned until 1861 when all Choctaw schools were closed at the beginning of the Civil War.

The Rev. Wright also organized the Wheelock Church in December 1832 with several members of the Mississippi church. Membership in the church increased steadily, and worship services were held in a small log cabin until a church of stone was built between 1844 and 1847.

In 1842 the Choctaw General Council enacted legislation creating a national education system to consist of a day and boarding schools to serve both boys and girls.

> By 1834 a new tribal constitution was produced and officials elected to govern the Choctaw people. The missionaries had opened schools and organized churches with the support and cooperation of their Choctaw friends.

Recovery from the Trail of Tears

THE CHOCTAWS HAD OCCUPIED a raw forested land and the most immediate need was to build homes, which they proceeded to do. They were a resilient people and they wasted no time in self-pity or seeking retribution for the ills they had suffered.

In the first few years in the new land, both the Choctaws and their missionary friends were plagued by illness in the form of fevers and respiratory ailments. Hundreds died, including many children and elders. Little medical help was available except for what the missionaries such as Rev. Wright and Cyrus Byington were able to provide.

By 1834 a new tribal constitution was produced and officials elected to govern the Choctaw people. The missionaries had opened schools and organized churches with the support and cooperation of their Choctaw friends. Small day schools were located near the mission stations where the majority of the settlers lived. These schools were managed by the missionaries and financed by their eastern support groups. Within ten years the Choctaws had managed to recover from the trauma of Removal, and by 1842 they had a school system and a functioning government.

A New Wheelock

IN 1882 THE CHOCTAW General Council authorized the creation of a new boarding-type school in the vicinity of the old Wheelock mission station. Four new buildings were constructed to house and serve Choctaw orphans. The construction was completed in 1884 and fifty orphans were the initial occupants. The school was staffed and managed by Presbyterian missionaries from 1884 to 1893, funded by Choctaw appropriations and mission support groups.

In 1893 the Choctaw Nation assumed control of the school and continued to run it until 1898. From 1898 to 1910 administration of the school was contracted to other entities. In 1910 the federal government assumed a greater role in the operation of the school and many improvements were made in the management and curriculum of the institution.

In 1932 the federal government enacted legislation placing the Bureau of Indian Affairs (BIA) in charge of Indian education. The BIA funded and managed the school until it closed in 1955 as a result of the federal policy that aimed to move Native American students into the public schools.

Over the course of Wheelock's long history (1832 to 1955), the physical plan of the school was significantly expanded and modernized. Girls from other Native American groups were also enrolled.

Several of the historic buildings at Wheelock still remain, although most are not open for public use. LeFlore Hall has been remodeled into a museum and is filled with artifacts and photographs.

▶▶ NOT FAR FROM WHEELOCK, IN SWINK, OKLAHOMA, THIS FOUR-ROOM LOG CABIN IS THE OLDEST HOUSE IN THE STATE. THE US GOVERNMENT BUILT IT FOR DISTRICT CHOCTAW CHIEF THOMAS LEFLORE, ACCORDING TO THE 1830 TREATY OF DANCING RABBIT CREEK. THE HOME WAS RESTORED IN 2003 AND IS LISTED ON THE NATIONAL REGISTER OF HISTORIC PLACES.

▶ BALL PLAY CEREMONY WHISTLES, COLLECTED 1908. Courtesy of the National Museum of the American Indian Cultural Resources Center, (018845.000).

CHIEF LeFLORE'S HOUSE

CHOCTAW: A CULTURAL AWAKENING

A CULTURAL AWAKENING

◀ Group of Choctaws at Smithsonian's National Museum of the American Indian. The Choctaw Nation of Oklahoma was the first to host a tribal festival at the museum.

37

CHOCTAW: A CULTURAL AWAKENING

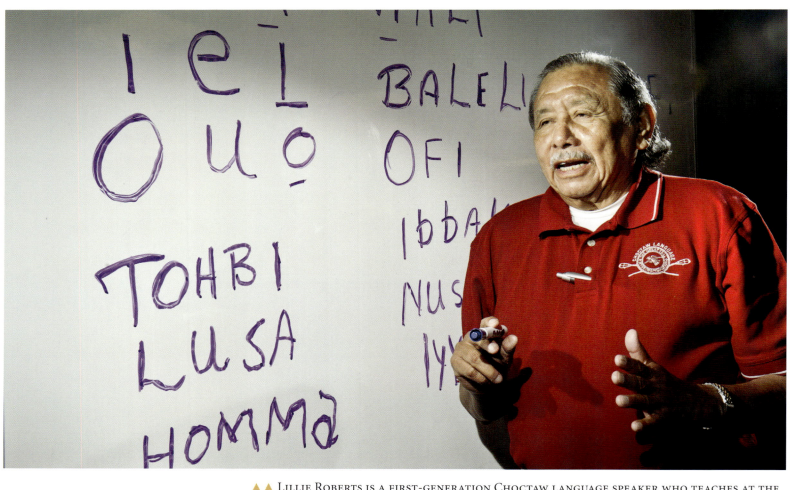

▲▲ Lillie Roberts is a first-generation Choctaw language speaker who teaches at the School of Choctaw Language. She is shown here teaching a class through the Internet.
▲ Choctaw language expert Richard Adams.

A CULTURAL AWAKENING

▲ Storyteller Tim Tingle entertaining visitors at the National Museum of the American Indian. He is the author of several award-winning books as well as being a celebrated performer.

CHOCTAW: A CULTURAL AWAKENING

◀ Greg Rodgers enjoys sharing legends and stories with audiences of all ages. He is pictured here in Washington, D.C., as a featured storyteller.

▼ Tracy Horst, Lisa Reed, Lana Sleeper, Judy Allen, Vonna Shults, Kay Jackson, and Sue Folsom in front of the Choctaw Days posters at the National Museum of the American Indian (NMAI) in Washington, D.C. This Choctaw leadership team, along with Dr. Ian Thompson, worked with the Smithsonian NMAI team to plan the first Choctaw festival at NMAI.

A CULTURAL AWAKENING

▶ Suzanne Heard was the first Princess of the Choctaw Nation in 1957. She is pictured holding the same basket she carried when chosen to represent the Choctaw Nation as "royalty." The portrait at her feet shows her soon after the pageant. Young ladies today are chosen during the annual Choctaw Nation Labor Day Festival to serve the tribe for a one-year reign as Princess.

▲ Counterclockwise from upper left: Basket in Progress, collected in 2000. Courtesy National Museum of the American Cultural Resources Center, (261928.000); Basket circa 1910. Kate McClendon Collection. Courtesy of the Oklahoma History Center and the Oklahoma Historical Society, (02613); Choctaw Mississippi Basket with large handles. Purchased in 1950. Courtesy of the National Museum of the American Indian Cultural Resources Center, (218641.000); These two Baskets were Collected in 2000. Courtesy of the National Museum of the American Indian Cultural Resources Center, (266814.000). ▶ Choctaw Museum Director Regina Green displays a portion of the basket exhibition at the Capitol at Tvshka Homma.

▲ Eveline Steele is an accomplished basket weaver in the traditional manner. She harvests river cane locally for her basketry.

▶ Teresa and Curtis Billy with many cultural and art ideas they use in sponsoring programs about Choctaw culture.

CHOCTAW: A CULTURAL AWAKENING

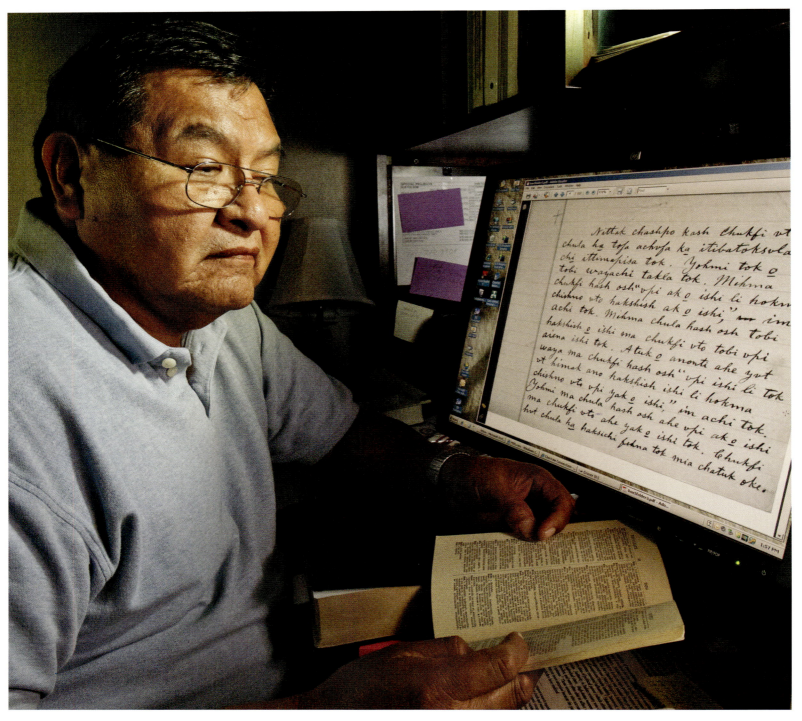

▲ OLIN WILLIAMS SERVES THE CHOCTAW PEOPLE IN HISTORIC PRESERVATION AND AS A RELIGIOUS LEADER. HE IS PICTURED IN HIS OFFICE COMPARING FABLES WRITTEN IN THE CHOCTAW LANGUAGE IN THE 1800S TO CONTEMPORARY ENGLISH-LANGUAGE VERSIONS OF THESE STORIES SO THAT HE CAN BE CERTAIN NOTHING IS LOST IN TRANSLATION.

▶ MISSISSIPPI CHOCTAW STICKBALL CAP WITH A WHITE FEATHER, COLLECTED IN 1908. COURTESY OF THE NATIONAL MUSEUM OF THE AMERICAN INDIAN, CULTURAL RESOURCES CENTER.

A CULTURAL AWAKENING

▲ Stickball exhibitions are an annual event at the Choctaw Labor Day Festival. Teams also compete in tournaments each year at the Tvshka Homma festival and at the world championship games in Philadelphia, Mississippi.

▶ Brad Joe, Choctaw singer and chanter.

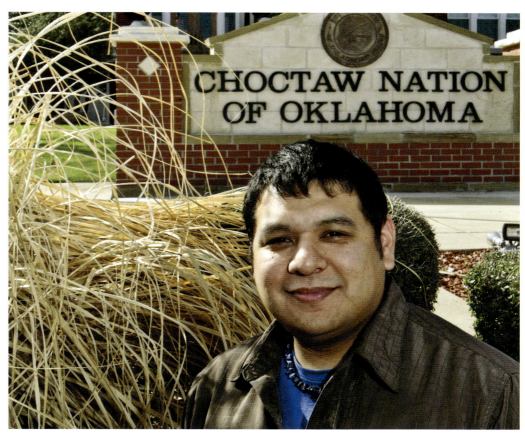

CHOCTAW: A CULTURAL AWAKENING

▲ Pictured at Choctaw Cultural Enrichment Camp learning basket weaving are Kanda Jackson, Kylee Anderson, Isabelle Cox, and Phillip Stevens. Sports camps are also held during the summer for youth interested in golf, basketball, football, stickball, and baseball.

CHOCTAW: A CULTURAL AWAKENING

▲ Each year, the Choctaw Nation hosts a Cultural Enrichment Camp, sharing stories, crafts, and activities to enrich the knowledge of the tribal heritage. The youth are shown here learning to make basic pottery. Pictured working with clay are (clockwise from upper left) Kenslee Folsom, Josephine Gilmore, Emily Stevens, and Athena Stallard.

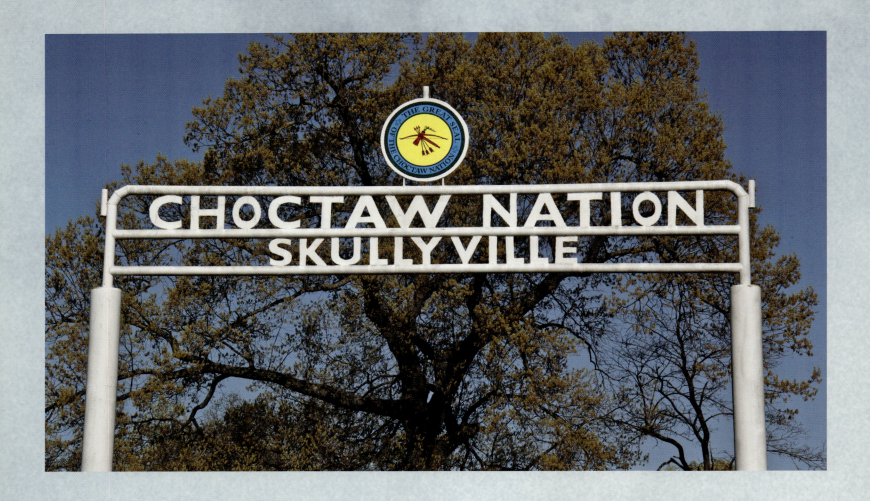

Skullyville was one of the first towns established after the Trail of Tears.

▶▶ The Oklahoma Historical Society signed over the deed to the Skullyville cemetery to the Choctaw Nation in May 1993. The Tribe fenced the property and erected an entrance sign to the "Choctaw Nation Cemetery."

Skullyville: Once Flourishing, Now at Rest

Skullyville, Oklahoma, was originally a part of Moshulatubbee District, which was located in what is now LeFlore County. This was one of the first towns established after the Trail of Tears. Because annuities were paid to the displaced tribal members from the Choctaw Agency run by the US government, the settlement name comes from the Choctaw word for money, *iskvli*, which eventually was anglicized to skully and joined with the French word "ville," to become Skullyville, or Money Town.

The Choctaw Nation Cemetery is located here, although it is historic only—interments no longer occur. In the mid-1800s, Skullyville was the largest town in Choctaw Nation—it was once the tribal capital. Now, the cemetery is the solitary landmark of the once thriving station.

The significance of this cemetery prompted the leaders of the Tribal Nation to take over the ownership and care of the property from the Oklahoma Historical Society in 1993, and since then the Nation has fenced, maintained, and tended this important part of tribal history.

Council Speaker Delton Cox lives nearby and has an avid interest in the culture and language of the Choctaw Nation. He is very proud of the heritage of the Tribe, and it is important to Speaker Cox that our ancestors are honored.

SCULLYVILLE CEMETERY

◀ Weatherworn tombstones date burials from the mid-1800s through the 1990s. Two former Choctaw chiefs are buried here, Governor Tandy Walker and Chief Edmund McCurtain. Visitors are welcome to tour the cemetery, although there are no new interments allowed.

▶ One gravestone clearly marks the final resting place of a Trail of Tears survivor.

▲ District 4 Tribal Council member Delton Cox has served his peers many years as Speaker of the Council. Knowledgeable on many aspects of tribal history, Delton is an advocate of education in the Choctaw language and culture. He and his wife live in LeFlore County only a few miles from the old town of Skullyville. He is pictured here at Skullyville Cemetery near a memorial erected by the Tribe shortly after the Choctaw Nation took over the property.

3

FOUNDATION OF FAITH

BUILT ON THE SOLID ROCK

As soon as Choctaw people arrived in their new homeland, they began building homes and planting crops, and they also prioritized establishing churches and schools. Christian missionaries, friends to the Choctaws, had made the long, sad march along the Trail of Tears with them in 1831.

Today, the fruits of their labor can be seen and heard—many of the places of worship built decades ago are still used in Christian services today. The revival of the tribal language has ensured that Choctaw hymnbooks are once again commonly used in services as tribal people express their love and appreciation for God through song. The New Testament and several books in the Old Testament are also translated and printed in the Choctaw language.

◀ Painting in Holy Rosary Catholic Indian Mission Church, Mississippi.

▲ Rev. Virginia Espinoza with her dissertation written and published in 2001, "The Spiritual Growth and Mission in the Choctaw Church: The Struggle of Choctaw Christians with Identity," the Ten Commandments translated into Choctaw, a Choctaw Hymnal, and a Choctaw Testament.

Choctaw Church Convention

ELEANOR CALDWELL

▲ Eleanor Caldwell with her painting of an old church campground.

◄ The Johnson Family Singers were the featured Choctaw gospel group performing at the Smithsonian festival in both 2011 and 2012. Bubba Johnson, Lena Scott, and Moses Johnson are invited to sing at many church functions.

The painting depicts an era in which the church was the central focus for the Choctaw families. Not only was it a place of prayer, Bible teaching, and taking care of the flock, but also a place to socialize by attending the functions the churches planned. Christianity is still prevalent among the people today, but the Choctaw churches are not the center of strength they once were. There has been a decline in attendance in the last twenty years or so. There are still a few operating with fewer families attending. The socializing today in the church is mostly "singings." Announced through newspapers and by word of mouth, these church socials include supper, congregational, group, and solo singing in celebration of events or to commemorate someone's life.

The Choctaws held their church conventions differently from the non-Indians. In this painting, they are having their three-day weekend meeting. The meeting would begin with a Friday evening meal, a time of worship, and open for business with a roll call of delegates sent from as many as fourteen local churches. The local churches

CHOCTAW: A CULTURAL AWAKENING

▲ Rev. Nathan Scott with wife, Linda, and grandson, Joseph Den Pah-she-ka Easley, Aiden Kanalli John, Loa Mae John, and Jimmie Scott at the Coal Creek Cumberland Presbyterian Church.

▶ Panki Bok Cumberland Presbyterian Church, outside of Eagletown, Oklahoma.

▶▶ Rev. Nathan Scott standing outside Coal Creek Cumberland Presbyterian Church holding his Bible.

operated within circuits or groups. The main departments, such as Sunday school, singing, etc., had separate conventions where the local churches came together for business.

A weekend church meeting was exciting, but it took a lot of planning and budgeting by the church as well as personnel, to host the gathering. The men would get busy building and repairing and chopping wood. The women would start washing and collecting quilts and pillows, and washing down the church floor and pews. The children would help with the work, but if they could get away with it, they would go play.

FOUNDATION OF FAITH

CHOCTAW: A CULTURAL AWAKENING

Families from the local church would move into the camp houses with their beds and beddings, dishes, pots and pans, groceries, and personal items about a week before the meeting and prepare everything that was to be used. They would not move back home until the meeting was over. Some families, who did not have a place to live, were allowed to live in these camp houses rent free. They fed their share of visitors, who were assigned to certain camps for their meals the entire weekend. Whenever someone wanted coffee, the person's assigned camp would accommodate them. Each camp was assigned an even number of visitors so that no one camp became overloaded.

Visitors would arrive with the intention of staying the weekend. Accommodations were a must as some traveled many miles to be there. Sleeping arrangements were the church floor, parsonage, and nearby family homes whose owners were away camping. In the wintertime, after the evening church business dismissed on Friday and Saturday nights, all the church pews were carried outside to make room for beddings. The women would spread quilts on the floor on one side for the women and on the other side for the men. After the lamps were put out for the night, the storytelling began. Jovial laughter would be heard until sleep overtook them.

It was early to rise and late to bed for both visitors and campers. The day began with an early morning cold face wash out in the open under a tree prepared for the visitor. A washstand was a small platform built into a tree. A bucket of water with a dipper, a bar of soap, a towel, and a mirror hung on a nail from the tree completed the lavatory. Next on the agenda was a prayer meeting before breakfast. By this time a person should be fully awake for breakfast, which surely they were.

From the camps arose the aroma of bacon, home-ground sausage, and strong coffee. Campers would always kill a hog for fresh meat to feed throughout the meeting. It wasn't considered a good feed without banaha (shuck bread), which is cornmeal balls wrapped in corn shuck and boiled in water, and a batch of fresh pork chunks fried in a huge cast-iron wash pot over an open fire. Choctaws will travel miles just to be able to eat this combination of their favorite foods. This explains why, on Sunday of such a meeting, people came in abundance. It was also a time to visit with people they hadn't seen in a while.

After the lamps were put out for the night, the storytelling began. Jovial laughter would be heard until sleep overtook them.

◄ AND ▲ CHOCTAW NATION TRIBAL COUNCILMAN THOMAS WILLISTON REPRESENTS DISTRICT 1, INCLUDING THE SOUTHERN PART OF MCCURTAIN COUNTY. HE IS PICTURED AT THE OLD WHEELOCK CHURCH NEAR MILLERTON. THIS CHURCH IS JUST OUTSIDE THE GATE OF THE WHEELOCK ACADEMY GROUNDS.

CHOCTAW: A CULTURAL AWAKENING

A favorite place to hang out at these meetings was the pop stand, especially for the young folks. During the meeting the stand would remain closed, but as soon as it dismissed, the people would converge upon it to quench their thirst and to visit. The stand sold ice-cold sodas, candy, and gum. It was usually built under a shade tree. The main item in the stand was the Coke box. The big red box was long and deep enough to hold many bottles of sodas and chunky chipped ice, which had been flaked off a big block of ice. That's the way ice was sold. The young folks hung out there knowing they could visit or flirt without getting into trouble with their strict parents. At least until the sexton rang the church bell, indicating it was time for service.

The services, under the brush arbor in the summertime, were full of power and conviction. There would be beautiful singing. Singing in one's native tongue causes one to feel a surge of inner strength and power. The congregation, resounding strongly throughout the countryside, sang songs in beautiful harmonious a cappella. Non-Indian neighbors of the church for miles around would hurry to finish their evening chores so they could sit on their front porches and listen to the singing. They didn't understand the words being sung, but they understood—through the Spirit—the worship and praise. The word of God preached with compassion, also in the native tongue, brought forth conviction to the listeners. With tears streaming down their faces, people both young and old would come and give their hearts to the Lord.

This painted story illustrates the enduring strength of the Choctaws, which cannot be found in history books.

▲ BISHOP STEVEN CHARLESTON IN THE SANCTUARY OF ST. PAUL'S CATHEDRAL IN OKLAHOMA CITY, OKLAHOMA.

◄ PASTOR HANNAH BRYAN AT THE 100-YEAR-OLD ROUND LAKE CUMBERLAND PRESBYTERIAN CHURCH LOCATED A MILE AND A HALF SOUTHWEST OF COALGATE, OKLAHOMA.

CHOCTAW: A CULTURAL AWAKENING

▼ Retired Presbyterian preacher Gene Wilson in his home outside Cache, Oklahoma. Wilson is one of the people credited with the revival of Choctaw dance and culture. He helped bring the teaching of Choctaw social dances to Oklahoma from Mississippi in the 1970s and '80s and is still called upon today for heritage foundational clarifications as well as Christian guidance.

▲ David Wilson, Conference Superintendent of the United Methodist Church, on the campus of Oklahoma City University.

A Brief History of Choctaw Hymns

VIRGINIA ESPINOZA

A person steps into a small Choctaw church and for the first time hears the people as they sing a Choctaw hymn, unknown to the stranger. If the person is not a Choctaw speaker the hymn will have no meaning, and will not be understood. It is like the hymns the European missionaries sang to the Choctaw people; they were not understood so they had no meaning until the new language was learned. A hymn is a song of love to their Creator. Sometimes the hymn reflects the pain of the Savior and the cruelty of the people. Other times it reflects what the needs of the people are.

In another time and place, it was soldiers hearing the Choctaw people as they left their homes and familiar places to begin their long march to a foreign land. One of the soldiers wrote in his journal that, "It is like a long continuous revival, the people sing from early morning until the last one goes to sleep at night." They were in constant communion with their Savior.

One of the hymns that the Choctaw people sing is "Meditation on Death." This song is often misunderstood. The title can be misleading, but it is a hymn of hope and anticipation. It reflects the person's understanding that he/she wasn't meant to stay here forever and that someday they will leave this place and go to the promised place. Another favorite is a hymn titled "Give Me Christ, or Else I Die." This hymn reflects the strong desire of the people to serve God with their whole being.

> *It is a hymn of hope and anticipation. It reflects the person's understanding that he/she wasn't meant to stay here forever and that someday they will leave this place and go to the promised place.*

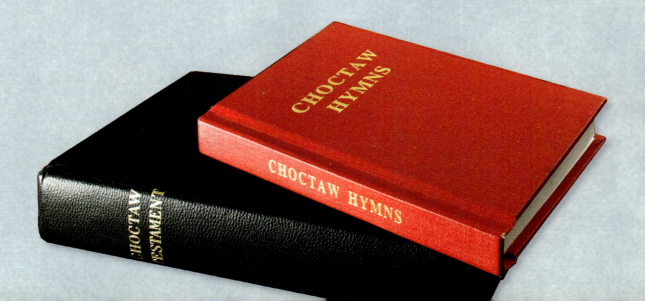

Choctaws Helped the Irish Famine Victims in 1847

Choctaw people have a history of helping others—one of the best examples is the $170 that was given to the people of Ireland in 1847 during the potato famine. To comprehend the beauty and generosity of this story, one has to understand how challenging the two preceding decades had been for the Indian people.

In 1831 the Choctaw Indians were forcibly removed from their ancestral lands to what is now known as Oklahoma. The Choctaws were the first of several Tribes to make the journey along the Trail of Tears.

The winter of 1831 was the coldest on record—the food and clothing of the men, women, and children sent along the Trail of Tears were severely inadequate and transportation needs were not properly met. Many Choctaws perished, and those who survived faced hardships establishing new homes, schools, and churches.

A few years after this long, sad march, the Choctaws learned of families starving to death in Ireland. Only sixteen years had passed since the Choctaws themselves had faced hunger and death on the first Trail of Tears, and they felt a great compassion toward the Irish people. Individual Choctaws made donations totaling $170 in 1847 to assist those suffering from famine in Ireland. These gracious Choctaw people, who had such meager possessions, gave generously to others in greater need.

The people of Ireland have never forgotten the pure humanity shown by the Choctaw Indians. The Irish, realizing that these Native Americans had delved deep into their own pockets for what little they had to share, have welcomed delegations from the Choctaw Nation and have visited the tribal lands in Oklahoma. In 1992, a plaque was unveiled at the Lord Mayor's Mansion in Dublin, Ireland, that reads, "Their humanity calls us to remember the millions of human beings throughout our world today who die of hunger and hunger-related illness in a world of plenty."

Individual Choctaws made donations totaling $170 in 1847 to assist those suffering from famine in Ireland. These gracious Choctaw people, who had such meager possessions, gave generously to others in greater need.

4
Beauty in Many Forms

CELEBRATING ART AND CULTURE

Appreciation of beauty is evident in the artifacts of Choctaw ancestors. Pottery, beadwork, baskets, clothing, and even the designs of the weapons, villages, and homes were more than functional—they were attractive as well. Attention to the details of design, color, and texture were important to Choctaw men and women—just as they are today.

Symbolism of designs was often important. For example, the basic pattern of the cotton dresses and shirts worn today as "traditional" clothing was adopted from the French. The diamonds on the clothing symbolize the diamondback rattlesnake to show a consciousness for nature and awareness that people must be careful to treat our surroundings with respect, caution, and prudence. Some dresses have four rows of ruffles to represent the four directions, others may have three rows to represent the three great chiefs: Apukshunnubbee, Pushmataha, and Mushulatubbee. And some dresses have only two rows of ruffles, simply because it is the dressmaker's personal preference. The styles of clothing change with each generation of creative Choctaw people, yet basic elements of design remain.

The Choctaw Nation is fortunate to have a tremendous number of talented writers, seamstresses, artists, and performers. Beauty truly does come in many forms. An Artist Registry for Choctaws may be found at www.choctawnation.com.

▶ Choctaw royalty representing the Tribe for 2011–12: Little Miss Summer Moffitt, Junior Miss Adrianna Curnutt, and Miss Choctaw Nation Amber Nicole Tehauno.

CHOCTAW: A CULTURAL AWAKENING

▲ Santa Fe artist Marcus Amerman has work on display in museums across the nation, including the Smithsonian. His work includes beads, glass, and performance art.

▶ Sue Folsom, the Executive Director of Cultural Services and Historic Preservation, is working on beading crowns for the princess pageants. Sue completes about eighteen crowns a year including the ones for the Okla Chahta event in Bakersfield, California. Her artistic talents go far beyond beadwork. She is also accomplished at pottery, painting, and basketry.

▲ Choctaw Princesses for 2010–11. Little Miss Mahala Battiest, Junior Miss Nikki Amos, and Senior Miss Kristie McGuire.

▶ Miss Indian Oklahoma for 2010–11, Dayla Amos of Broken Bow, Oklahoma.

Arrows: Beautifully Engineered Weapons

IAN THOMPSON, PHD

The traditional arrow is part of a complex weapon that also includes the bow and bowstring. All three must be finely tuned to each other to work effectively. To produce an accurate shot, the arrow itself must have the correct length and stiffness for the particular bow that it is fired from; the arrow must be the right weight, and this weight must be properly balanced to keep it from tumbling; the arrow must have the correct aerodynamics to fly straight; and the tip must be properly suited to its intended function. A traditional arrow is a deadly weapon, no question about it, but it is also very much a piece of art.

In the Choctaw language, an arrow is known as "oski naki," or "iti naki." The first term translating literally as "cane projectile" is used if the arrow shaft is made from river cane. The second term, translating as "wooden projectile," is used if the shaft is made from any type of wood.

Archived editions of *BISKINIK* on ChoctawNation.com contain in-depth articles about the Choctaw bow and arrow in action (January 2010), Choctaw "arrowheads" (July 2011), the process for making a traditional Choctaw bow (October 2010), making arrows (March 2012), and making a Choctaw war arrow (April 2012).

▶ Deadly Southeastern war arrows.
Photo © 2012 President and Fellows of Harvard College, (99-12-10/52972, 99-12-10/52973, and 99-12-10/52974).

CHOCTAW: A CULTURAL AWAKENING

▲▲ Carole Ayers is comfortable painting at her lake house at Kingston, Oklahoma. She enters her completed canvas at shows throughout the year including the Labor Day Art Show at Tvshka Homma.
▲ Paintings by Gwen Coleman Lester often depict Choctaw heritage. She studies the history of the Tribe so that her art can depict the culture with accuracy.

▼ Choctaw traditional potter Edmon Perkins has won many awards for his creations. He is pictured here in his studio with his dog, Katie.

▲ Choctaw flute maker Presley Byington from Idabel, Oklahoma. Presley shares Choctaw traditions with others through dance, music, and stories.

▼ D. G. Smalling pictured with his glass tipi art. Smalling works with jewelry and glass, but is best known for his line art, sketching in a single line without ever lifting pen from paper.

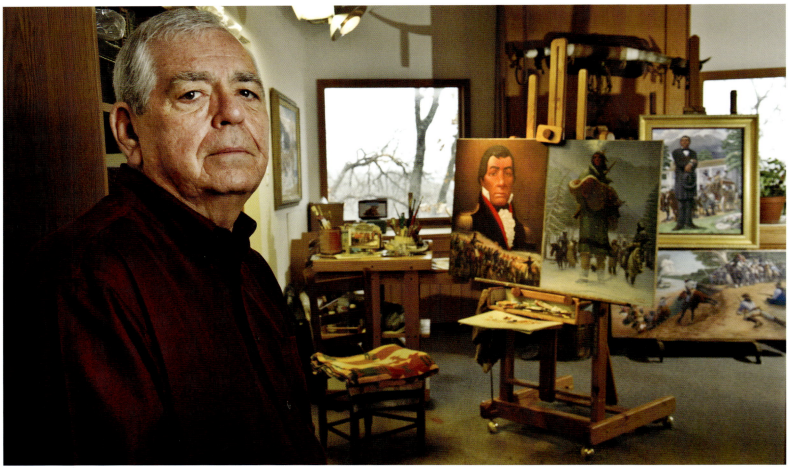

▲▲ Paul Hacker creates one-of-a-kind knives and flutes, as well as pottery and ledger paintings. His beautiful flute music is available on CD.
▲ Choctaw artist Neal Taylor with paintings in his home in Durant, Oklahoma.

BEAUTY IN MANY FORMS

▼ CHESTER COWEN, RETIRED FROM THE OKLAHOMA HISTORICAL SOCIETY WHERE HE WAS EMPLOYED FOR MANY YEARS AS THE PHOTO ARCHIVIST, IS PICTURED SURROUNDED BY SOME OF HIS BEAUTIFUL BEADWORK AND CULTURAL COLLECTIONS.

▲ Artist Dylan Cavin in his Norman, Oklahoma, studio. His award-winning art has gained the attention of Tribe and state, earning him an invitation to show his work at the Oklahoma State Capitol during Choctaw Days and also earning the honor

BEAUTY IN MANY FORMS

▼ Jane Semple Umsted helped begin the annual art show at Tvshka Homma. She has a studio in Durant, Oklahoma, and enjoys sharing the history of the Tribe through art.

▲ Author and playwright LeAnne Howe is the winner of the Tulsa Library Trust 2011 American Indian Festival of Words Author Award. She was named winner of the Lifetime Achievement Award from the Native Writers' Circle of the Americas in 2012.

BEAUTY IN MANY FORMS

▼ Choctaw artist Kathy Sturch of Durant, Oklahoma, has a reputation for painting stunning images of people. The annual art show at Tvshka Homma has been fortunate to receive her entries.

85

BEAUTY IN MANY FORMS

▲ AND ▶ TERESA JEFFERSON AT HOME IN TISHOMINGO, OKLAHOMA, SEWING A CHOCTAW SHIRT FOR HER SON, JOSEPH. SHE MADE HER FIRST CHOCTAW DRESS IN 1980.

◀ KNOWN TO MANY AS PRINCESS PALE MOON BECAUSE OF THE HONORARY TITLE GIVEN BY WILLIAM A. DURANT IN 1940, YVONNE LYONS HUSER HAS BEEN RECOGNIZED OFTEN FOR HER BEAUTIFUL SCULPTURES AND PAINTINGS. SHE IS PICTURED IN HER STUDIO IN HOLDENVILLE, OKLAHOMA.

▲ Nancy Southerland-Holmes shows the Pendleton blanket she designed with the stickball theme, "Little Brother of War." This Choctaw-designed Pendleton was a limited edition and is no longer available for purchase.

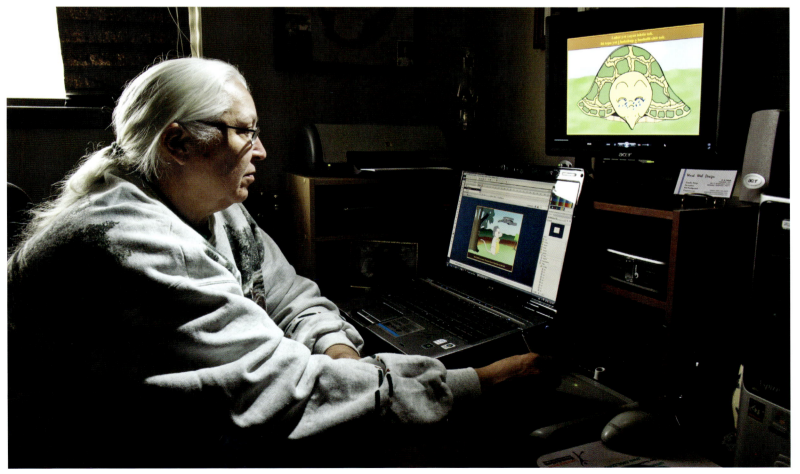

▲▲ Mary Bever from Davis, Oklahoma, provided the artwork for the 2010 Commemorative Trail of Tears Walk.
▲ P. K. Work concentrating in her home studio in Stillwater, Oklahoma, on a cartoon animation of a traditional Choctaw story "How Turtle Got Cracks in His Shell."

CHOCTAW: A CULTURAL AWAKENING

▲ Double-woven red and tan river cane basket collected in 2000. Courtesy of the National Museum of the American Indian, (266816.000).

◄ Rose Billy weaves Choctaw designs into baskets. She displays her talent each year at the Choctaw Village during the Labor Day Festival at Tvshka Homma.

► Lyman Choate works on his wood sculptures at his home in Hochatown, Oklahoma.

BEAUTY IN MANY FORMS

CHOCTAW: A CULTURAL AWAKENING

▲ Professor Devon Mihesuah has authored many books. Shown here are some of the titles. She won the 2012 Oklahoma Writers' Federation Trophy Award for Best Work of Fiction for her fifteenth book, *Document of Expectations* (Michigan State University Press.) Previous awards include the Oklahoma Writers' Federal Trophy Award for Best Non-Fiction and the Oklahoma Historical Society's Award for Outstanding Book on Oklahoma History.

▶ Dr. Clara Sue Kidwell is an author and historian, and is formerly the Director of Native American Studies at the University of Oklahoma. She took on the challenge of beginning the American Indian Center at the University of North Carolina in 2007. She has served as the Associate Dean of Program Advancement at Bacone College in Muskogee, Oklahoma, since 2011.

BEAUTY IN MANY FORMS

▼ Beadwork artist Roger Amerman with some of his extraordinary projects, including a beaded leather jacket, displayed at the National Museum of the American Indian during Choctaw Days.

BEAUTY IN MANY FORMS

◄ AND ► SILVERSMITH HARRY JAMES IN TALIHINA, OKLAHOMA. HIS CREATIVE WORK CAN BE FOUND AT THE CHOCTAW NATION'S GIFT SHOP AT TVSHKA HOMMA.

◄ SHELLY WESTBROOK IS WORKING ON GOURD ART IN HER STUDIO AT MCALESTER, OKLAHOMA.

CHOCTAW: A CULTURAL AWAKENING

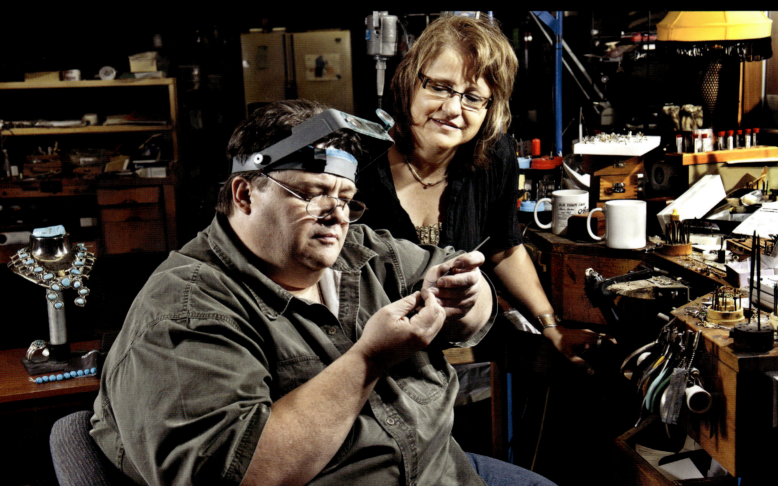

▲▲ Theresa Renegar, jewelry artist. Her unique designs are often made from natural stone and metals.

▲ Jeweler Chris Sewell and Theresa Renegar working together in Chris's jewelry store in McAlester, Oklahoma.

BEAUTY IN MANY FORMS

◄ AND ▲ WOOD-CARVER JACK HAYNES FROM MCALESTER, OKLAHOMA, IS A "REGULAR" AT THE SENIOR CITIZEN'S LUNCHEONS AT THE CHOCTAW COMMUNITY CENTER. SOME OF HIS AMAZING ARTWORK IS ON DISPLAY IN THE OFFICES AT THE CENTER, AND HE KEEPS BUSY AT HOME CREATING BEAUTIFUL CARVINGS FROM FOREST GLEANINGS.

CHOCTAW: A CULTURAL AWAKENING

▲ Verna Todd with traditional Choctaw pottery she has created.

▲ D. J. Battiest-Tomasi with one of the flutes she uses in therapy with patients at the Oklahoma City Indian Clinic. She represented Choctaw culture in Washington, D.C., at the John F. Kennedy Center in 2011 with her flute when she and storyteller Tim Tingle were invited to perform at an event. D. J. has a master's degree in Behavioral Studies.

5

Chahta Warrior Pride

TVSHKA HOMMA

▲ Ruth McMillan, daughter of WWI Choctaw Code Talker Tobias Frazier.

◄ Lt. Col. Bobby Yandell, 45th Infantry Brigade Combat Team, standing in front of the Veterans Memorial in Oklahoma City, Oklahoma.

Choctaw Code Talkers were the original code talkers of World War I—the first to use their Native language during wartime to transmit coded messages. Their success was so phenomenal that other Native Americans were sought after and trained as code talkers in both World War I and World War II; Choctaws provided this invaluable service in both wars. Actions of these telephone warriors were a military secret for many years, so federal recognition has been long overdue. In 2008, the Code Talkers Recognition Act was signed into law, providing a Congressional Medal to Tribes with code talkers.

Choctaw leaders are very appreciative of the men and women who serve in the military, and have given approval to various programs that show support. The Choctaw Nation is part of a team providing free flights to wounded veterans and their families for medical and other compassionate purposes through a national network of volunteer pilots and aircraft. Veterans of Operation Iraqi Freedom and Operation Enduring Freedom (Afghanistan) are a priority for the Veterans Airlift Command.

Lighthorsemen of the Choctaw Nation Upheld the Law

BILL COLEMAN SR.

▲ Edith Billy is the widow of WWII Choctaw Code Talker Schlicht Billy. She is pictured holding his photo and medals. Lt. Billy was in Company F of the 180th Infantry of the 45th Division. He was awarded the Silver Star with oak leaf cluster, the Purple Heart with three oak leaf clusters, Presidential Unit Citation, and battlefield commission.

◄ Major General Rita Aragon (retired), Secretary of Veterans Affairs for Oklahoma.

All Five Civilized Tribes had some type of police force from the late 1700s until after the Civil War. In 1818, soon after the missionaries went to Mississippi and established schools in their northern district, the Choctaws had their first mounted police. Their duties were to ride over each district to settle disputes in family matters and to arrest all who violated the law. At the start, they performed their duties much like a county sheriff and later were patterned much like the Texas Rangers, having a Captain and several enlisted men.

In October 1821, many old customs in the Choctaw Nation were set aside and a new system of policing the Nation was established.

In the Northeast District of Mississippi the new police force was called Lighthorsemen. And Lighthorsemen were exactly what the name indicated. Their

CHOCTAW: A CULTURAL AWAKENING

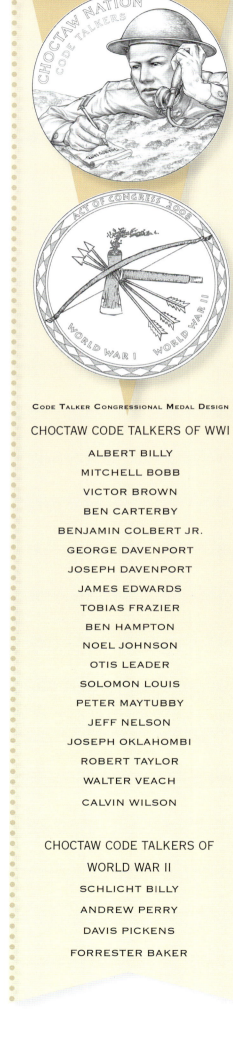

CODE TALKER CONGRESSIONAL MEDAL DESIGN

CHOCTAW CODE TALKERS OF WWI

ALBERT BILLY
MITCHELL BOBB
VICTOR BROWN
BEN CARTERBY
BENJAMIN COLBERT JR.
GEORGE DAVENPORT
JOSEPH DAVENPORT
JAMES EDWARDS
TOBIAS FRAZIER
BEN HAMPTON
NOEL JOHNSON
OTIS LEADER
SOLOMON LOUIS
PETER MAYTUBBY
JEFF NELSON
JOSEPH OKLAHOMBI
ROBERT TAYLOR
WALTER VEACH
CALVIN WILSON

CHOCTAW CODE TALKERS OF WORLD WAR II

SCHLICHT BILLY
ANDREW PERRY
DAVIS PICKENS
FORRESTER BAKER

regular equipment was a horse, saddle, rifle, and revolver, for they were a hard-riding, hard-fighting group of men who carried no excess provisions. As they moved swiftly from place to place in search of criminals, they subsisted on a few handfuls of parched corn and beef jerky, stuffed in their pockets or saddlebags.

Greenwood LeFlore became a district Chief in 1821, and under his influence and that of others, the Choctaw Nation made some great strides in the abolishment of many of their primitive practices. It was soon after his election that the Choctaws modified their district organizations and adopted a system of tribal legislation and a code of written law.

The Choctaw custom of allowing murderers to be disposed of by relatives of the dead man or woman was set aside. Murderers, thieves, whiskey peddlers, and all other offenders had the same right to trial by the Lighthorsemen, who acted in a three-fold capacity—sheriff, judge, and jury. They were brave, tough men and as they rode the countryside, nothing escaped their watchful eyes. They soon became a terror to white whiskey peddlers and other intruders who invaded the Choctaw Nation.

CHAHTA WARRIOR PRIDE

And Lighthorsemen were exactly what the name indicated. Their regular equipment was a horse, saddle, rifle, and revolver, for they were a hard-riding, hard-fighting group of men who carried no excess provisions.

◀ OIL PAINTINGS OF WWI CODE TALKERS JOSEPH OKLAHOMBI AND OTIS LEADER PAINTED BY FR. GREGORY GERRER O.S.B. THE PAINTINGS WERE A GIFT TO THE MABEE-GERRER MUSEUM OF ART IN SHAWNEE, OKLAHOMA, BY MRS. SELTON JONES-SEMEAN JACKSON, MRS. SILSAINEY JONES JOHNSON, MRS. NELLIE SAMUEL STECHI, AND MRS. EMILINE COLBERT BAKER. COURTESY OF THE MABEE-GERRER MUSEUM OF ART.

▼ THESE PISTOLS, CIRCA 1850, ARE ATTRIBUTED TO CHIEF PETER PITCHLYNN. COURTESY OF THE OKLAHOMA HISTORY CENTER AND THE OKLAHOMA HISTORICAL SOCIETY, (01264.2.1 AND 01264.2.2).

Lighthorsemen proved they were worth their weight in gold during the Removal from the east. They kept strict control of the masses and prevented many of their kin from falling into the hands of highwaymen during their long march to the west.

After reaching their new home in the west, they found the conditions far worse from what they had been used to. They were taking possession of a land that was already occupied by several different Indian Tribes and groups of white settlers of the worst character. When the US Congress created the Indian Territory, it generated many more problems for the Tribes and their police forces. Upon its creation, it became a nation within a nation, where no US court had jurisdiction, and no Indian court had jurisdiction over any white man or woman. Indian Territory became a perfect hideout for all types of riffraff looking for a refuge from the law. The Civil War brought more hardships for Indian Territory. Both the North and the South left it unprotected and vulnerable to all sorts of raiders and outlaws. However, at the close of the Civil War, the United States moved in a direction to correct this situation. It created a court for the Western District of Arkansas and gave it jurisdiction over Indian Territory.

▶ OVERLEAF: WWII VETERANS AT THE ANNUAL CEREMONY HONORING THEIR SERVICE. THEY ARE PICTURED WITH CHIEF GREGORY E. PYLE, ASSISTANT CHIEF GARY BATTON, LT. GENERAL LEROY SISCO (RETIRED), ARMY CAPTAIN TERRI SCROGGINS, AND REV. BERTRAM BOBB.

▲▲ THE CHOCTAW CAPITOL BUILDING WAS CONSTRUCTED IN 1884 AND HAS BEEN IN CONTINUOUS USE. IT IS CURRENTLY UTILIZED AS A TRIBAL COURT, A MUSEUM, AND GIFT SHOP. THE TRIBAL COUNCIL MEETS IN CHAMBERS ACROSS THE ROAD.

▲ WWII HERO ALVIE N. CARNEY WAS AWARDED THE SILVER STAR AND IS A SURVIVOR OF IWO JIMA.

Even though their Nation had its share of bootleggers, murderers, horse thieves, and holdup men, the Choctaws had very good control of its citizens and white population, in part because the citizens of the Nation respected the judicial powers of the Lighthorsemen. Although they were stripped of much of these powers at a later date, they remained a very effective peacekeeping force until statehood in 1907.

Occasionally, the Choctaw Lighthorsemen joined forces with deputies of the US Marshals offices in Fort Smith to rid the territory of notorious gang members and whiskey peddlers. Indian Territory was dry, and the white man's whiskey caused more deaths than any other act of lawbreaking.

The Choctaw law stated that if any person refused to allow his "ardent spirits" to be destroyed by the Lighthorsemen, he did so at his own risk. In many cases the whiskey peddler refused, or simply provoked a gun battle and made a run for it, which resulted in deaths on each side. Noncitizens who held permits to work, ranch, or farm had to abide by the same laws as the Choctaw citizens. Oftentimes, permit holders came into direct conflict with the Lighthorsemen, resulting in the loss of their permits and expulsion from the Choctaw Nation.

Sometimes the Lighthorsemen stepped over their jurisdiction and dealt severely with outside molestation, especially when noncitizens were in violation of pistol laws, whiskey peddling, and resisting arrest. In many of these incidents

▶ KOREAN WAR HERO TONY BURRIS WAS KILLED IN ACTION ON OCTOBER 9, 1951, AT THE AGE OF TWENTY-TWO. HE WAS POSTHUMOUSLY AWARDED THE CONGRESSIONAL MEDAL OF HONOR. THE CHOCTAW NATION SPONSORED THIS STATUE TO RECOGNIZE BURRIS IN HIS HOMETOWN OF BLANCHARD, OKLAHOMA.

▶ Overleaf: Councilmen Perry Thompson, Jack Austin, Anthony Dillard, Thomas Williston (kneeling), Delton Cox, James Frazier, Bob Pate (kneeling), and Joe Coley at Chief Pushmataha's grave at Congressional Cemetery in Washington, D.C. When Pushmataha passed away in 1824, he asked that the "big guns be fired over him," and was granted a twenty-one-gun salute.

CHOCTAW: A CULTURAL AWAKENING

▲ WWI Code Talker Ben Hampton's photograph is displayed by his grandchildren Delores Marshall, Michael Halcomb, Denny Halcomb, and Royce Halcomb.

▶▲ Descendants of WWI Code Talker Tobias Frazier: Katie McCoy, Dara McCoy, Luke Clay, Lacy Clay, Beth Lawless, Olivia Clay, and Chantelle Standefer.

involving noncitizens, death occurred, and the Choctaw Nation had to defend their Lighthorsemen in federal court.

In some cases, the Lighthorsemen were harshly criticized for their crude practice of execution and severely inhuman treatment of persons in their custody, but in most cases their own Nation's laws protected them.

The Lighthorsemen were loyal, dedicated men, willing to put their lives at risk every day against robbers, murderers, drunkards, and bootleggers. Many of these brave men lost their lives in an attempt to disarm or arrest a crazed, misguided renegade filled with rotgut whiskey.

Fortunately, statehood did not end the career of all of the Lighthorsemen. Many of these courageous men became members of local police forces, county sheriffs, and deputy US Marshals.

Even today, it is not uncommon to find descendants of former Lighthorsemen working in law enforcement agencies throughout the state of Oklahoma, standing beside their brothers and sisters fulfilling a mandate handed down by their forefathers many years ago.

CHAHTA WARRIOR PRIDE

▲ CHIEF GREGORY E. PYLE AND PUBLIC RELATIONS EXECUTIVE JUDY ALLEN WORKING ON THE CONGRESSIONAL MEDAL DESIGN FOR THE CODE TALKERS OF WWI AND WWII. THE LEGISLATION FOR THE MEDALS WAS SIGNED INTO LAW IN 2008 AFTER MANY YEARS OF WORK TO OBTAIN FEDERAL RECOGNITION FOR NATIVE AMERICAN CODE TALKERS. SEE DESIGN ON PAGE 104.

CHOCTAW: A CULTURAL AWAKENING

CHAHTA WARRIOR PRIDE

◀▲ Choctaw Nation pilots Al Cherry (sitting), John Wesley, and Quentin McLarry volunteer for Veterans Airlift Command and the Tribe furnishes use of the aircraft for the worthy cause. They are pictured at the Flight Operations in Durant.

◀ The Veteran's Advocacy Program does many things to assist people currently serving in and retired from the military. One of the projects that keep the advocates busy is sending hundreds of care packages each month to the soldiers who are overseas. Just after this picture was taken, most of these advocates were deployed to serve our country. All returned home safely. All four are active servicemen and deserve our gratitude. From left to right, Brent Oakes, Kelly McKaughan, John Lance, and Jason Burwick.

▲ Choctaw Defense is the nation's leading Native American defense manufacturer, producing a wide variety of military and commercial products. CEO Steve Benefield leads a team that engineers and manufactures many of the items from the ground up in this unique tribal business.

CHOCTAW: A CULTURAL AWAKENING

CHAHTA WARRIOR PRIDE

CHOCTAW: A CULTURAL AWAKENING

◀ Overleaf: A portion of the Choctaw Nation Color Guard: John Moffitt, Rhonda Willmott, Shirley Mantaghi, Terry Loman, Joseph O'Brien, Nellie Hunter, Melvin Tom, Bob Ludlow, Sampson Moore, Audie Gibson, John Burleson, John Barry, and Herbert Jessie.

▶ Rhonda Willmott at her great-great-grandfather's allotment land. Rhonda, a veteran of the US Army, is a member of the Choctaw Nation Color Guard.

▶▶ Nellie Hunter serves as a member of the Color Guard and is always proud to display her veteran's status. She lives in Tupelo, Oklahoma.

CHAHTA WARRIOR PRIDE

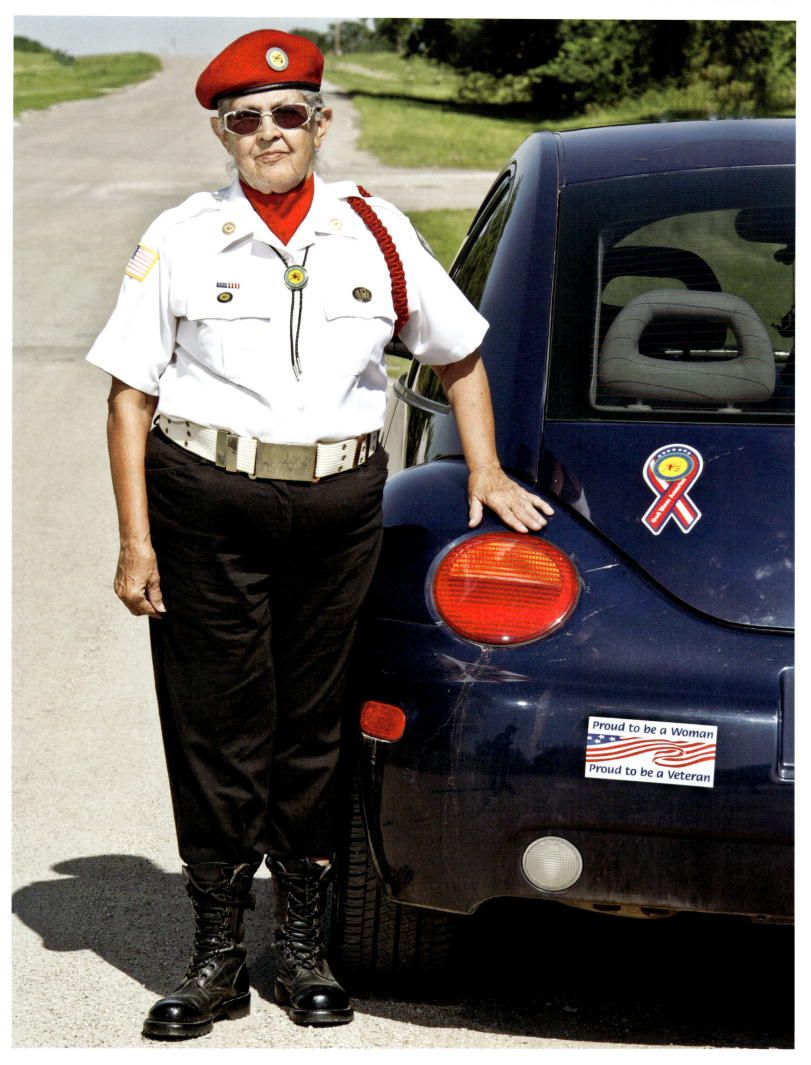

CHOCTAW: A CULTURAL AWAKENING

▲ SHIRLEY MANTAGHI PROUDLY STANDS IN FRONT OF THE WAR MEMORIAL AT POTEAU, OKLAHOMA. SHE HAS SERVED IN THE CHOCTAW COLOR GUARD FOR FOURTEEN YEARS.

▶ HERBERT JESSIE, CHOCTAW COLOR GUARD COORDINATOR.

CHOCTAW: A CULTURAL AWAKENING

▲ Col. Tray Ardese pinned by his wife, Tammy, on his most recent promotion.
◀ Assistant Chief Gary Batton and Chief Gregory E. Pyle at former Choctaw Chief Pushmataha's gravesite. Pushmataha is one of only two Choctaw chiefs buried at Congressional Cemetery in Washington, D.C. Peter Pitchlynn is also buried there.
▶ Councilman Kenny Bryant, like many others who serve as Tribal Council Members, once served in the US military. Kenny is a veteran of the army and is a member of the Choctaw Veterans Association. He is pictured here in downtown Talihina, Oklahoma.

CHAHTA WARRIOR PRIDE

▲ Public Safety Executive John Hobbs leads a department for the Choctaw Nation that features a high-tech environment, the collaboration of efforts between tribal officers and city and county officers, and a tremendous education component, especially with the DARE (Drug Abuse Resistance Education) program.

◂◂ Bill Coleman spent much of his life sharing what he learned about the history of the Choctaws, including the fascinating story of the Lighthorsemen.

◂ Sylvester Moore, Sergeant-at-Arms for the Choctaw Tribal Council since 1999.

6

Tribal Services and Systems

ENDURING SINCE THE FOUNDATION OF OUR GOVERNMENT

Ever-improving opportunities have been made available to tribal members and communities throughout Choctaw Nation. In addition to grants from the federal government, the leaders of the Tribe have wisely invested in business developments that produce revenue to provide services for education, health, elder programs, family and social services, and much, much more.

Sophisticated tribal courts, historic preservation offices, state-of-the-art clinics, and a new hospital have given Choctaw people tremendous advantages in improving the standard of living for their families.

▲ Tribal Councilman James Frazier and elders from District 12. The senior citizens from the Choctaw Community Centers in Crowder and Coalgate are on a bus trip to San Antonio.

◄ Choctaw Nation Tribal Chaplain Bertram Bobb is a former Speaker of the Choctaw Council. In 2010 he was presented with a Lifetime Achievement Award by the Choctaw Nation.

The Final Choctaw Dawes Commission Rolls

BRENDA S. HAMPTON

The Five Civilized Tribes were removed from their homelands of Alabama, Mississippi, and Louisiana and relocated to Indian Territory (Oklahoma) beginning around 1830. The Dawes Commission Rolls were opened in the Oklahoma territory in 1899 and compiled through 1906, with the exception of an Act of Congress that opened the rolls for one additional day in 1914.

In order to enlist on the Final Dawes Rolls, applicants had to prove to the Dawes Commission that they were of Indian (Choctaw) descent. In some cases this meant having relatives and friends swear that they were of Indian ancestry. One's color and ability to speak the language were also factors considered prior to acceptance by the Dawes Commission and for allotments of land or money.

Many applicants were not accepted for reasons unknown to us today. Some of the instances for denial that have been discovered are that the individual did not remain in residence in Oklahoma, weren't the right color, couldn't speak their language, or were at one time on the rolls but passed away before they were closed and their names were stricken.

▲ Choctaw Judges David Burrage, Mitch Mullin, and Fred Bobb pictured in the Tribal Courtroom at Tvshka Homma.

◄ Brenda Hampton, the former Executive Director of Tribal Membership, CDIB, Voter Registration, and Photo ID. Mrs. Hampton served the Tribe from 1985 until her death in 2011. She is pictured with three government-issued Dawes Rolls books.

CHOCTAW: A CULTURAL AWAKENING

▲ Choctaw Court System Judges Pat Phelps, Marion Fry, Mitchell Leonard, and (seated) Steven Parker.

◄ Former Judge Juanita Jefferson served the Choctaw Nation for almost twenty-three years before she retired. She passed away March 30, 2011.

The Final Approved Dawes Commission Rolls closed March 4, 1907, by the Act of Congress of April 26, 1906 (34 Stat. 137). The Final Rolls have about 18,809 names listed as Choctaws by blood and 1,643 Mississippi Choctaws of Oklahoma by blood. These totals include thirty-eight names that were added on August 1, 1914.

It is our understanding that the first Certificate of Degree of Indian Blood (CDIB) was issued by the US federal government through the Department of Interior/Bureau of Indian Affairs (BIA) in 1942. The Choctaw Nation of Oklahoma contracted the CDIB program from the BIA in July of 1986. We adhere to the federal regulations set forth for issuing CDIB cards. The Tribe does the research, inputs all of the information determining lineage, and attaches the appropriate documents for submission to the BIA for approval or denial.

▲ Historic Preservation staff Skylar Robinson with Assistant Chief Gary Batton using ground penetrating radar equipment to locate graves in an old cemetery site. This was especially relevant to the Assistant Chief since some of his ancestors were buried at this cemetery. "It is exciting to witness the use of state-of-the-art technology in finding information about our past," said Batton.

The rolls are used to assist individuals in proving their Choctaw lineage. In order to do this they must connect back to a direct ancestor (such as a parent, grandparent, great-grandparent, etc.) who enrolled by blood with the Final Dawes Commission Rolls. It is the applicant's responsibility to obtain the required legal documentation proving connection to the direct ancestor who was enrolled. The only documents that are used by the Choctaw Nation CDIB/Tribal Membership Office and accepted by the Bureau of Indian Affairs are state issued full-form birth and death certificates.

When the Tribe contracted the issuance of CDIBs, there were approximately 35,700 Choctaws with CDIB cards proving their Choctaw lineage. By late 2011, records showed more than 200,000 Choctaws with CDIB cards.

Brenda Hampton served in the Choctaw Nation of Oklahoma CDIB/Tribal Membership Department from 1985 through 2011.

TRIBAL SERVICES AND SYSTEMS

▲ Georgia Mae Self of Antlers was the last living original enrollee in the Choctaw Nation. Born on October 21, 1904, she was 106 years old when she passed away on June 27, 2011.

CHOCTAW: A CULTURAL AWAKENING

▶ THE TRIBAL COUNCIL IN EACH DISTRICT ENSURES THE NEEDS OF YOUTH AND ELDERS ARE MET THROUGHOUT THE YEAR. DISTRICT 11 COUNCILMAN BOB PATE IS SHOWN HERE WITH YOUNG PEOPLE FROM HIS DISTRICT AS THEY WRAP CHRISTMAS PRESENTS FOR THE ANNUAL PARTY. HIS HELPERS ARE SHELDON TEAGUE, CHERISH WILKERSON, KELSIE ROACH, CALLIE MORRIS, DANETTA WILKERSON, (FRONT ROW) MIRANDA LALLI, AUSTIN BREGGS, AND CLAYTON TEAGUE.

TRIBAL SERVICES AND SYSTEMS

TRIBAL SERVICES AND SYSTEMS

◀ AND ▲ A BEAUTIFUL HOSPITAL IN TALIHINA IS CONTINUALLY BEING UPDATED, AND CLINICS IN STIGLER, HUGO, BROKEN BOW, MCALESTER, IDABEL, POTEAU, AND ATOKA HELP NATIVE AMERICANS ACCESS HEALTH CARE ACROSS THE CHOCTAW NATION. COUNCILMAN RON PERRY FROM DISTRICT 5 IS PICTURED AT THE STIGLER HEALTH CLINIC AND LONGTIME DISTRICT 8 COUNCILMAN PERRY THOMPSON IS AT THE HUGO WELLNESS CENTER.

CHOCTAW: A CULTURAL AWAKENING

▲ Teresa Jackson, Director of the Choctaw Nation Health Care Center, at the MRI exam room in Talihina.

▶▲ Executive Director of Choctaw Nation Outreach Randy Hammons presents a holiday basket filled with food for a Thanksgiving meal to Priscilla Coleman.

▶ McAlester Dental Clinic with Dr. Richard Howell, DDS and Assistant Leigh Ann Fassino and patient.

TRIBAL SERVICES AND SYSTEMS

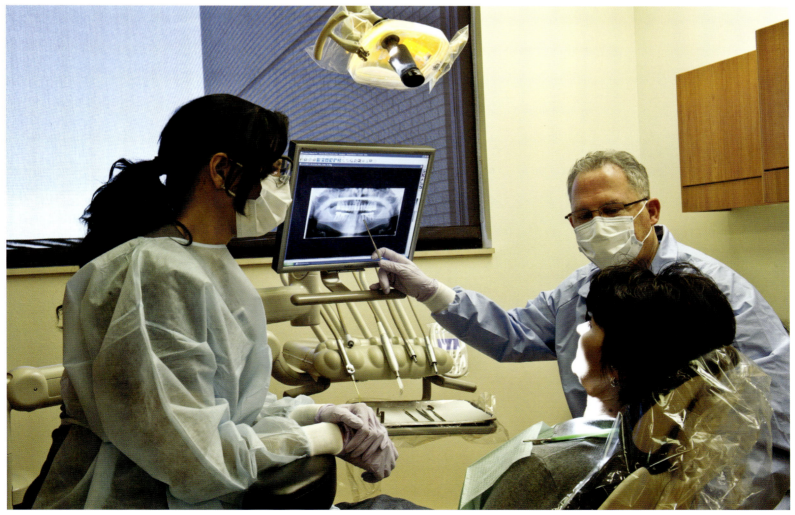

TRIBAL SERVICES AND SYSTEMS

◀ District 10 Tribal Councilman Anthony Dillard enjoys talking to his area seniors and visitors as they create beautiful beadwork and clothing items. Pictured with Anthony are Naomi LeFlore-Weakley, Sue Crowley, Bonita Martin-Price, December Pittman, Charlene Lloyd, and Nehemiah Gipson.

CHOCTAW: A CULTURAL AWAKENING

▼ Shannon McDaniel, Executive of Tribal Management, is pictured with Benny Robison, Kim White, and Lari Ann Brister discussing the Children and Family Services Program.

TRIBAL SERVICES AND SYSTEMS

◄ BISKINIK assistant editor Larissa Copeland and editor Lisa Reed checking press runs. The monthly newspaper is mailed to more than 81,000 homes and is also available at www.choctawnation.com.

▲ Chief Gregory E. Pyle at the Choctaw Nation Recycle Center in Durant. The Recycle Center is one of the Tribe's "going green" efforts that Chief Pyle has spearheaded in recent years. He has led the charge for the Choctaw Nation to become more environmentally conscious, and as a result the Tribe has won several state awards.

7
A Taste of Choctaw

SHARING THE SAVOR

▲ Lorene Blaine prepares fry bread at her home in Bryan County.
◄ Adeline Hudson, pounding corn the traditional way. Food and cooking exhibits (with samples!) are always prominent at the Choctaw Village during the Labor Day Festival at Tvshka Homma.

Crops were an important part of the Choctaws' life. Tribal ancestors were experts at raising agricultural treasures such as corn, squash, beans, and pumpkins. The women, elders, and children of the Tribe were gatherers of what the earth produced in field and forest and were able to provide for the families' tasty meals. The food was cultivated and gathered on a seasonal basis.

Combined with the meat and fish provided from the hunting prowess of the men and boys of the Tribe, Choctaws of the past had a nice variety of food to choose from. Shellfish was also eaten, and the discarded shells were used in making jewelry and crushed to mix with clay for pottery.

The pottery that the Choctaws made was very beautiful and extremely useful. Today, the art of making the clay pottery with early designs and firing it in an open fire is still being practiced by Oklahoma Choctaws. In a unique cultural trade of educating

A TASTE OF CHOCTAW

◀ Tribal Councilman Joe Coley shows wild onions that have been picked near Red Oak to prepare a specialty dish of eggs and onions. Fourche Maline Creek at Robbers Cave State Park is in the background. Choctaws look forward to the wild onion feast at the tribal community center in Wilburton each spring.

▶ Charisse Ladd and Willie Walley hoeing the garden planted by the elders at the Choctaw Community Center at Durant. The fresh vegetables are used at the lunches served each week to the elders, and surplus is available to the senior citizens for home use.

147

CHOCTAW: A CULTURAL AWAKENING

▶ A TRADITIONAL HOG FRY IS COOKING SALT PORK IN A LARGE CAST-IRON POT OVER AN OPEN FIRE. THE MEAL IS SHARED WITH FAMILY AND FRIENDS. COUNCILMAN KENNY BRYANT SHOWS HOW TO STIR THE MEAT AS IT COOKS.

Grape Dumplings

½ gallon unsweetened grape juice
2 cups sugar

Dumplings:
1 to 1½ cups water
4 tablespoons shortening, melted
2 teaspoons baking powder
2 cups flour
1 teaspoon salt

Bring grape juice to a rolling boil with the sugar. Mix water, shortening, salt, and baking powder in a medium bowl. Add enough flour to make a stiff dough. Turn the dough out onto a floured board, and roll out to ½-inch thickness. Cut dough into small pieces with a knife. Drop each dough piece one at a time into the boiling juice. Cook over high heat uncovered about 5 minutes. Then lower heat and simmer for about 15 minutes with cover on. Plate and serve. This dish can be garnished with whipped cream.

Makes 6 to 8 servings

Tanchi Labona

2 cups pearl hominy corn
2 pounds pork backbone (country ribs work well)
2 to 3 quarts water
Salt to taste, approximately 4 tablespoons

Have water in large pot ready. Pick through your hominy corn for any debris and then rinse well before cooking. Place corn, pork, water, and salt in pot and cook on low for seven to eight hours, until corn is done. A slow cooker (crock-pot) works well with this recipe. Remember to stir frequently to keep the corn from sticking to the bottom of the cooker.

Makes 12 to 14 servings

Wild Onions and Eggs

Wild onions, cut up (approximately 2 pounds or 2 large handfuls)
1 cup water
1 cup shortening, melted
6 eggs

Cut up wild onions to fill a 6- to 10-inch skillet. Place water, shortening, and onions in the skillet. Salt to taste and simmer until almost all the water is gone (15 to 20 minutes). With a fork, lightly beat the eggs in a small bowl then pour on top of onions, stirring well. Cook until the eggs are scrambled. Serve hot.

Makes 4 to 6 servings

▶ An elbow-shaped basket woven from river or swamp cane, collected in 1950. This shape of basket was often used for collecting and separating herbs. Courtesy of the National Museum of the American Indian, Cultural Resources Center, (251361.000).

TRADITIONAL RECIPES

▲ Vonna Shults (right) and Shirley Barboan cooking rabbit gumbo at the National Museum of the American Indian.

▲ Betty Ketchashawno and son Cedric preparing pashofa and banaha at the traditional village at Tvshka Homma.

Banaha

- 2 cups cornmeal
- 1 teaspoon baking soda
- 1 teaspoon salt
- 1½ cups boiling water
- 8 corn husks (boil about 10 minutes before using)

Mix dry ingredients in medium bowl and then add water. Mixture should be stiff enough to handle easily. Form into oblong balls and wrap in corn husks. Tie in the middle with corn husk string. Drop into a deep pot of boiling water. Cover and cook for 40 minutes. Serve hot.

Makes approximately 8 servings

▶ Banaha, a favorite bread made by boiling a cornmeal mixture in a cornhusk wrap.

▶▶ Lorene Blaine displays a banquet of traditional food. On her table are delightful plates of banaha, fried pies, pinto beans, fry bread, tanchi labona, grape dumplings, and salt pork. She also serves a glass of iced tea to wash it all down.

▼ Buffalo horn spoon, circa 1812, Emma Christian Collection. Courtesy of the Oklahoma History Center and the Oklahoma Historical Society, (02500).

each other, the Oklahoma Choctaw Historic Preservation team is teaching the pottery making to the Mississippi Band of Choctaws and in return is learning the traditional art of gathering, stripping, and weaving baskets from river cane.

Before the cultural exchange program began in 2012, there were only a few truly traditional basket weavers in Oklahoma. Just as there has been a revival of Choctaw language, there is also a cultural awakening of our heritage in pottery, baskets, moccasin making, dance, archery, and many other forms of Choctaw customs and history. Yakoke (thank you) to all those who are sharing the traditions!

A TASTE OF CHOCTAW

153

CHOCTAW: A CULTURAL AWAKENING

▶ Sarah (Beloved) Sharp and Les Williston in the traditional Choctaw Village at the Capitol Grounds at Tvshka Homma. Beloved is displaying some fruit, nuts, and grains that have been harvested and preserved. Les constructed the chukka, or wooden living structure, that they are standing in. Visitors to the Tvshka Homma can walk through the village and see the structures.

8

Choctaw People from All Walks of Life

GROWING WITH PRIDE, HOPE, AND SUCCESS

Citizens of the Choctaw Nation have succeeded at life and careers all across the globe. This section is devoted to a small sampling of the diversity of the tribal people who have contributed their knowledge and talents to those around them. When challenged with scheduling photographs of Choctaws for this book, the list of those we wanted to include kept growing longer and longer. Teachers, legislators, elders, musicians, moms, dads, princesses, and cowboys—just to name a few careers representing the people we did manage to obtain portraits of. It would have been fulfilling to continue taking pictures of Choctaws for this enjoyable book assignment, but we simply ran out of time. And yet the pages of this book are filled with images of the remarkable people of our Tribe.

It is an honor and an inspiration to know them!

▲ Saddle maker Howard Council from Lawton is a National Cowboy and Western Heritage Hall of Fame inductee.

◀ Ernest and John A. Hooser on the remaining stairs of the storage building for the Tuskahoma Female Institute. Their family lived on the academy grounds from 1929 to 1931.

CHOCTAW: A CULTURAL AWAKENING

▲ Frank Watson is one of the people who worked on the Choctaw Constitution Committee to prepare the document the Choctaw Nation has operated under since 1983. He points to his signature on the historic document dated July 25, 1983.

▶ Choc Charleston opened the Choctaw Trading Post in Oklahoma City, Oklahoma, and operated it until his retirement.

CHOCTAW PEOPLE FROM ALL WALKS OF LIFE

▲ Professor Joe Watkins, Director of Native American Studies at the University of Oklahoma.

▲ Gena Timberman, Director of the American Indian Cultural Center and Museum, at the construction site of the new facility in Oklahoma City, Oklahoma.

A Vision Toward Education

▲ Tribal Councilman for District 9 Ted Dosh has served on the Choctaw Council longer than any other member; he has been steadfast as a servant leader for the Tribe since 1979. He is a tremendous proponent of education and is extremely happy to see the construction of the new Child Development Centers, which provide services to children and families.

▶ Director of Scholarship Advisement Program (SAP) Jo McDaniel holding the 2010 Drum Award presented for the innovative education assistance program. With Jo are SAP staff members Stephanie Gardner, Twauna Williams, and Shauna Williams.

Providing tools for self-sufficiency includes offering educational and training opportunities. The Choctaw Nation has parlayed success in business by utilizing revenues to create unique scholarship grants and career development programs for post–high school students, as well as significant academic achievement programs for younger students. The Choctaw Nation has Head Start Programs in fourteen towns, and has constructed a state-of-the-art classroom facility at the Jones Academy for grades one through six, which complements the amazing campus of the residential school that is home to about 180 children annually. A career-training program certifies tribal members for new or advanced careers, and the Success Through Academic Recognition program is available nationwide for grades two through twelve. Scholarship Advisement won a Drum Award in 2010, thanks to a nomination from Harvard, for their contributions in providing career, financial, and

EDUCATION

163

▲ Brad Spears has served as the director of Jones Academy since 1997. Grades one through six attend class on campus, and the older grades go to school at nearby Hartshorne, Oklahoma.

In 2012, Choctaw University was launched! This is a giant step in succession planning for the Tribe.

scholarship counseling to students, and helping with school retention at college and university.

And in 2012, Choctaw University was launched! This is a giant step in succession planning for the Tribe. The 100-year vision of the Chief includes training employees from within, and Choctaw U is a leadership and education program that helps meet that goal. These and the many other examples of tribal education and career development programs show that many advanced opportunities are accessible.

▶▲ The Choctaw Nation headquarters building in Durant, Oklahoma, houses administrative offices for the Chief and many programs of the Tribe. Offices located across the Choctaw Nation have staff available to offer one-on-one assistance to tribal members.

▲ Executive Director of Education Joy Culbreath has organized many projects during her tenure, including the School of Choctaw Language, a tremendous adult education program, improvements to the Jones Academy campus, and an academic program at Jones Academy. She has also led initiatives such as new scholarship programs and a Jones Academy Foundation. These are all components of the 100-year vision of the Tribe.

EDUCATION

EDUCATION

▲ Rachel Ouellette was a student at Goodland. Her trip as a child for medical care at a hospital in Talihina, Oklahoma, helped inspire her to become a nurse. Rachel has traveled the world but now lives in Virginia and enjoys writing about her memories as a young girl.

◀ The entrance to Goodland School. Founded by early Presbyterian missionaries in 1848, the school is located near Hugo, Oklahoma, on a rural 390-acre campus. Goodland Academy remains a private Christian school that provides an excellent education for students K-12.

▶ Choctaw doll, collected 1964.
Courtesy National Museum of the American Indian Cultural Resources Center, (234895,000).

CHOCTAW PEOPLE FROM ALL WALKS OF LIFE

◄ Oklahoma State Representative Lisa Johnson Billy with her husband, Phillip; son, Masheli, with his flute; youngest son Nahinli; and daughter Anoli, who served as Little Miss Indian Oklahoma City in 2012.

► Oklahoma State Representative Mike Christian is proud to be a tribal member.

CHOCTAW: A CULTURAL AWAKENING

◀ OKLAHOMA STATE REPRESENTATIVE DUSTIN ROBERTS WAS ELECTED IN 2010 TO SERVE DISTRICT 21. HE IS A VETERAN OF THE US NAVY.
▶ OKLAHOMA STATE SENATOR AL MCAFFREY. HE SERVED 5½ YEARS AS A STATE REPRESENTATIVE AND WAS ELECTED IN 2012 AS A SENATOR.

CHOCTAW PEOPLE FROM ALL WALKS OF LIFE

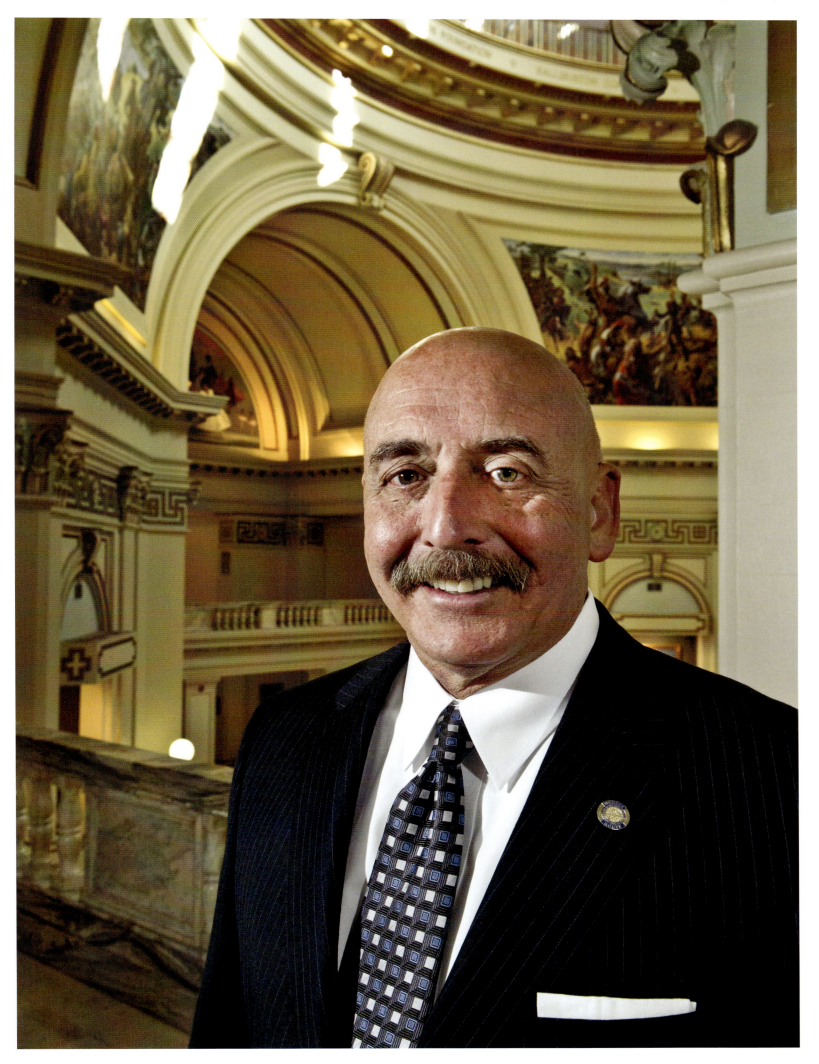

CHOCTAW: A CULTURAL AWAKENING

▲ Oklahoma State Senator Josh Brecheen. He was elected to state leadership in 2010.

▶ Oklahoma State Representative Seneca Scott. The Choctaw Nation is fortunate to have so many tribal members serving at the State Capitol.

CHOCTAW PEOPLE FROM ALL WALKS OF LIFE

CHOCTAW: A CULTURAL AWAKENING

▲ Bob West is a reporter for the *McCurtain County Gazette* in Idabel, Oklahoma

▶▲ V. W. "Buster" Jefferson inside the Oklahoma Choctaw Community Center. Buster was a primary force in getting the center started in Oklahoma City, Oklahoma.

▶ Robert Holden, deputy director of the National Congress of American Indians (NCAI) in the NCAI Embassy in Washington, D.C., stands in front of the mural of the members' first meeting in Colorado.

CHOCTAW PEOPLE FROM ALL WALKS OF LIFE

CHOCTAW: A CULTURAL AWAKENING

▲ Attorneys Mike Burrage (seated) and David Burrage with Oklahoma State Senator Sean Burrage.

▶ Claire Richard first presented the idea of Project Falvmmichi to the Choctaw Nation when she was sixteen years old. The anti-bullying program is a huge success and is in public schools across the 10½ counties, sponsored by the Tribe through the Youth Empowerment Program.

CHOCTAW: A CULTURAL AWAKENING

▲ Elder Laura Carney at her home in Smithville, Oklahoma. She was born December 26, 1912.

▶ Emeline Bohanon, born February 26, 1919, understands what she hears in English but only speaks in the Choctaw language. She is pictured here with the last quilt she made by hand. She lives in her home in Honobia, Oklahoma.

CHOCTAW PEOPLE FROM ALL WALKS OF LIFE

CHOCTAW: A CULTURAL AWAKENING

CHOCTAW PEOPLE FROM ALL WALKS OF LIFE

◄ Ida Crosby lives in Idabel, Oklahoma, and only speaks Choctaw.

► Suzanne Heard and Betty Watson display a photograph of their mother, Irene Hudson Heard, an original enrollee of the Choctaw Nation. Irene was the daughter of Peter Hudson, superintendent of the Tuskahoma Female Institute. Suzanne was the first Princess of the Choctaw Nation.

CHOCTAW PEOPLE FROM ALL WALKS OF LIFE

▲ Florence Spalding and her sister, Clara Isabel Clampet, are both active in programs at the Choctaw Center in Idabel, Oklahoma.

◀ R. D. Folsom at Chief Peter Pitchlynn's grave at Congressional Cemetery, Washington, D.C. Folsom is the great-great-great-grandson of Chief Pitchlynn.

▲ CHOCTAW ELECTION BOARD MEMBERS JUDY OGLE AND KAY GREEN.

▶▲ ONEIDA WINSHIP, A THIRTY-FOUR-YEAR EMPLOYEE OF THE CHOCTAW NATION, IS PICTURED WITH TRIBAL MEMBER LADORA DENNY AS THEY WORK ON ELDER ASSISTANCE PROGRAM ISSUES.

▶ DISTRICT 2 TRIBAL COUNCILMAN TONY MESSENGER IN FRONT OF FAMILY INVESTMENT CENTER, BROKEN BOW, OKLAHOMA.

CHOCTAW PEOPLE FROM ALL WALKS OF LIFE

CHOCTAW: A CULTURAL AWAKENING

CHOCTAW PEOPLE FROM ALL WALKS OF LIFE

▲ John Vietta, the driver for the Durant Fire Department, has been with the department for fifteen years and serves as an instructor at Oklahoma State University for rescue classes. Fire Chief Roger Joines has been with the Durant Fire Department for twenty-two years.

◄ Former Boswell Police Chief Isaac Sexton.

► Rainette Womack Rowland, in front of Pushmataha Hall at Wheelock, assisting David Fitzgerald with the photography for the *Choctaw: A Cultural Awakening* book project.

▲ Choctaw Casino Resort Hotel, Durant, Oklahoma.

CHOCTAW PEOPLE FROM ALL WALKS OF LIFE

▼ Choctaw Casino and Resort Executive Janie Dillard (front right), with team members (left to right) Tammy Gwin, Jeff Penz, and Misty Dillard.

CHOCTAW: A CULTURAL AWAKENING

CHOCTAW PEOPLE FROM ALL WALKS OF LIFE

◀ Special Programs Executive Jack Pate, Agriculture Director Jack Hicks, Field Supervisor Doyle Bacon, and Ranch Manager Cal Stewart standing in front of about 120 head of cattle on Lick Skillet ranch near Idabel, Oklahoma. Ranching is one of the businesses of the Choctaw Nation.

CHOCTAW: CULTURAL AWAKENING

▲ Brian McClain is Executive of Legislative Advocacy and Water Management for the Choctaw Nation. He works as tribal liaison with the legal team led by tribal attorneys Bob Rabon and Mike Burrage on water-related issues.

▶▲ Jack Austin Sr. serves District 7 as Choctaw Councilman. He is standing at Sardis Lake, Oklahoma, which is in his area.

▶ Jimmy Kirkes, Choctaw Ranch Manager at the Tvshka Homma, with the buffalo herd of thirty-seven cows, two bulls, and twenty-four calves.

CHOCTAW PEOPLE FROM ALL WALKS OF LIFE

CHOCTAW: A CULTURAL AWAKENING

▶ The Choctaw Natural Resources Committee at Kiamichi River, near Sardis Lake, Oklahoma. Chief Gregory E. Pyle, Dr. John Jackson, Judy Allen, Shannon McDaniel, Bill Blankenship, Angel Rowland, Brian McClain, Dana Bonham, Natural Resources Executive Director Wayne Wylie, Tye Baker, and Assistant Chief Gary Batton.

CHOCTAW PEOPLE FROM ALL WALKS OF LIFE

BIBLIOGRAPHY FOR AN INDIGENOUS CHOCTAW HISTORY

Adair, James
> 1775 *The History of the American Indians; Particularly those Nations Adjoining to the Mississippi, East and West Florida, Georgia, South and North Carolina, and Virginia.* Printed for Edward and Charles Dilly, London.

Anderson, David G. and Kenneth E. Sassaman
> 2004 Early and Middle Holocene periods, 9500–3750 BC. In *Handbook of North American Indians,* Vol. 14, edited by Raymond D. Fogelson, pp. 77–87. Smithsonian Institution, Washington, DC.

Baird, W. David
> 1973 *The Choctaw People.* Indian Tribal Series, Phoenix.

de Biedma, Luys Hernandez
> 1993[1544] Relation of the Island of Florida. Translated by John E. Worth. In *The De Soto Chronicles: The Expedition of Hernando de Soto to North America in 1539–1543*, Vol. I, edited by Lawrence A. Clayton, Vernon James Knight Jr., and Edward C. Moore, pp. 221–246. University of Alabama Press, Tuscaloosa.

Bushnell, David Jr.
> 1909 The Choctaw of Bayou Lacomb, St. Tammany Parish, Louisiana. *Smithsonian Institution Bureau of American Ethnology,* Bulletin 48. Government Printing Office, Washington, DC.

Cabeza de Vaca, Alvar
> 1905 *The Journey of Alvar Nunez Cabeza de Vaca and His Companions from Florida to the Pacific 1528–1536.* Translated from his own narrative by Fanny Bandelier. Trail Makers (series), New York.

Carleton, Kenneth H.
> 1994 Where Did the Choctaw Come From? An Examination of Pottery in Areas Adjacent to the Choctaw Homeland. In *Perspectives on the Southeast: Linguistics, Archaeology, and Ethnohistory*, edited by Patricia B. Kwachka. Southern Anthropological Society Proceedings, No. 27. University of Georgia Press, Athens.

Claiborne, John
> 1880 *Mississippi as a Province, Territory, and State: With Biographical Notices of Eminent Citizens.* Vol. I. Power and Barksdale, Jackson, MS.

Clayton, Lawrence A., Vernon James Knight Jr., Edward C. Moore, eds
> 1993 *The De Soto Chronicles: The Expedition of Hernando de Soto in North America in 1539–1543.* University of Alabama Press, Tuscaloosa.

DeRosier, Arthur H. Jr.
> 1970 *The Removal of the Choctaw Indians.* Harper & Row Publishers, New York.

Du Pratz, Antione Simon Le Page
> 2006[1758] *History of Louisiana: Or of the Western Parts of Virginia and Carolina . . .* BiblioBazaar, USA.

Elvas, a Gentleman from
> 1993[1557] True Relation of the Hardships Suffered by Governor Hernando De Soto & Certain Portuguese Gentlemen During the Discovery of the Province of Florida. Translated by James Alexander Robinson. In *The De Soto Chronicles: The Expedition of Hernando de Soto to North America in 1539–1543*, Vol. 1, edited by Lawrence Clayton, Vernon James Knight Jr., and Edward C. Moore, pp. 19–220. University of Alabama Press, Tuscaloosa.

Galloway, Patricia K.
> 1995 *Choctaw Genesis 1500–1700.* Indians of the Southeast Series. University of Nebraska Press, Lincoln.

Garcilaso de la Vega
> 1993[1596] La Florida. Translated by Charmion Shelby. In *The De Soto Chronicles: The Expedition of Hernando de Soto to North America in 1539–1543*, edited by Lawrence A. Clayton, Vernon James Knight Jr., and Edward C. Moore, pp. 25–560. University of Alabama Press, Tuscaloosa.

Gibson Jon L., and J. Richard Shenkel
> 1988 Louisiana Earthworks: Middle Woodland and Predecessors. In *Middle Woodland Settlement and Ceremonialism in the Midsouth and Lower Mississippi Valley*, edited by R. C. Mainfort Jr., pp. 7–18. Mississippi Department of Archives and History, Jackson.

Gibson, Jon L.
> 2001 *The Ancient Mounds of Poverty Point: Place of Rings.* University Press of Florida, Gainesville.

Green, Len
> 1978 How to Lose a Nation in Seven Not-So-Easy Treaties. *Bishinik* July:10–11. Durant, OK.

Halbert, Henry S.
> 1985[1899] The Sacred Mound of the Choctaws. *Mississippi Historical Society,* In *A Choctaw Source Book*, edited by John Peterson Jr., pp. 223–234. Garland Publishing, Inc., New York.

Hudson, Charles
> 1976 *The Southeastern Indians.* University of Tennessee Press, Knoxville.

Iberville, Pierre Le Moyne
> 1981[1702] *Iberville's Gulf Journals*. Translated by Richebourg McWilliams. University of Alabama Press, Tuscaloosa.

Jenkins, Ned J. and Richard A. Krause
> 1986 *The Tombigbee Watershed in Southeastern Prehistory*. University of Alabama Press, Tuscaloosa.

Kidwell, Clara Sue
> 2008 Choctaws and Missionaries in Mississippi Before 1830. In *Pre-Removal Choctaw History*, edited by Greg O'Brien, pp 200–220. University of Oklahoma Press, Norman.

Knight, Vernon James and Vincas P. Steponaitis
> 1998 A New History of Moundville. In *Archaeology of the Moundville Chiefdom*, edited by V. J. Knight and Vincas P. Steponaitis, pp. 1–26. Smithsonian Institution Press, Washington, DC.

Livingood, Patrick
> 2011 *Mississippian Polity and Politics on the Gulf Coastal Plain: A View from the Pearl River, Mississippi*. University of Alabama Press, Tuscaloosa.

Mangelsdorf, P. C., Richard MacNeish, and Gordon Willey
> 1964 Origins of Agriculture in Middle America. In *Handbook of Middle American Indians*. Vol. 1, Natural Environment and Early Cultures, edited by R. C. West. pp. 427–445. University of Texas Press, Austin.

Martin, Paul and R. G. Klein, eds.
> 1984 *Quaternary Extinctions: A Prehistoric Revolution*. University of Arizona Press, Tucson.

Morse, Dan F., David G. Anderson, and Albert C. Goodyear
> 1996 The Pleistocene-Holocene Transition in the Eastern United States. In *Humans at the End of the Ice Age: The Archaeology of the Pleistocene-Holocene Transition*, edited by Lawrence G. Straus, Berit Eriksen, Jon Erlandson, and David R. Yesner, pp. 319–338. Plenum Press, New York.

Perdue, Theda
> 1988 Indians in Southern History. In *Indians in American History*, edited by Frederick E. Hoxie, pp. 137–159. Harlan Davidson Inc., Arlington Heights, IL.

Pesantubbee, Michelene
> 2005 *Choctaw Women in a Chaotic World: The Clash of Cultures in the Colonial Southeast*. University of New Mexico Press, Albuquerque.

Purdy, Barbara
> 1992 Florida's Archaeological Wet Sites. In *The Wetland Revolution in Prehistory*, edited by Bryony Coles, pp. 113–124; proceedings of a conference held by the Prehistory Society and WARP at the University of Exeter, April 1991.

Rangel, Rodrigo
> 1993[ca. 1540] Account of the Northern Conquest and Discovery of Hernando De Soto. Drawn from *Historia General y natural de las Indias* by Gonzalo Fernandez de Oviedo y Valdes. Translated by John E. Worth. In *The De Soto Chronicles: The Expedition of Hernando de Soto to North America in 1539–1543*, edited by Lawrence A. Clayton, Vernon James Knight Jr., and Edward C. Moore, pp. 247–306. University of Alabama Press, Tuscaloosa.

Schuldenrein, Joseph
> 1996 Geoarchaeology and the mid-Holocene Landscape History of the Greater Southeast. In *Archaeology of the Mid-Holocene Southeast*, edited by Kenneth E. Sassaman and David G. Anderson, pp. 3–27. University Press of Florida, Gainesville.

Smith, Bruce D.
> 2006 Eastern North America as an Independent Center of Plant Domestication. *Proceedings from the National Academy of Sciences*. 103 (33): 12223–12228.

Swanton, John R.
> 1969 *The Indians of the Southeastern United States*. Smithsonian Institution Bureau of American Ethnology Bulletin, 137. Greenwood Press Publishers, New York.

Tolbert[1958], Charles Madden.
> 1975 A *Sociological Study of the Choctaw Indians in Mississippi*. Unpublished dissertation. Louisiana State University, 1958. Xerox University Microfilms, Ann Arbor, MI.

Webb, Thompson, Patrick J. Bartlein, Sandy P. Harrison, and Katharine H. Anderson
> 1993 Vegetation, Lake Levels, and Climate in Eastern North America for the Past 18,000 Years. In *Global Climate Since the Last Glacial Maximum*, edited by H. E. Wright Jr., et al., pp. 415–67. University of Minneapolis Press, Minneapolis.

Wright, Alfred
> 1828 Choctaws: Religious Opinions, Traditions, Etc. *Missionary Herald* 24: 178–183, 214–216.

Index

Adams, Richard, 38
Allen, Judy, 23, 40, 113, 194–95
Amerman, Marcus, 72
Amerman, Roger, 94
Amos, Dayla, 74
Amos, Nikki, 74
Anderson, Kylee, 49
Apukshunubbee (warrior Chief), 12, 13, 70
Aragon, Rita, Major General (Ret.), 102
Ardese, Tray, Colonel, 123
arrows, 75
art and culture: appreciation of, 70; arrows, 75; authors, 84, 92–93; basketry, 41–45, 48–49, 90; beadwork, 73, 81, 95; cartoon animation, 89; Choctaw Princesses, 70–71, 74; clothing and sewing, 87; flutes, 78, 80, 99; glass tipi art, 79; gourds, 94; jewelry, 96; Marcus Amerman, 72; painting, 59, 76, 80, 82, 83, 85, 86; pottery, 50–51, 77, 98; silversmithing, 95; stickball blanket, 88; wood sculptures and carving, 91, 97
Artist Registry, 70
atlatl, 22
Austin, Jack, 12–13, 15, 110–11
Austin, Jack, Sr., 193
authors, 84, 92–93
Ayers, Carole, 76

Baker, Tye, 194–95
ball play ceremony whistles, 34
banaha (shuck bread), 63, 151–53
Barboan, Shirley, 150
Barry, John, 116–17
basketry, 41–45, 48–49, 90, 149, 152
Battiest, Mahala, 74
Battiest-Tomasi, D. J., 99
Batton, Gary (Assistant Chief), 11, 15, 16, 23, 106–7, 122, 132, 194–95
beadwork, 73, 81, 95
Benefield, Steve, 115
Bever, Mary, 89
Billy, Anoli, 168
Billy, Curtis, 45
Billy, Lisa Johnson, 168
Billy, Masheli, 168
Billy, Nahinli, 168
Billy, Phillip, 168
Billy, Rose, 90
Billy, Schlicht, 103, 104
Billy, Teresa, 45
BISKINIK newspaper, 15, 75, 142
Black Belt Prairie, 21
black pottery bowl, 1
Black Warrior River, 25

Blaine, Lorene, 145, 153
Blankenship, Bill, 194–95
blankets, stickball blanket, 88
Bobb, Bertram, Reverend, 16, 106–7, 126
Bobb, Fred, 17, 129
Bohanon, Emeline, 179
Bonham, Dana, 194–95
bow and arrow, 12–13, 22
bowls, 1, 20, 24
breastplate, Mississippi Choctaw breastplate, 5
Brecheen, Josh, 172
Breggs, Austin, 134–35
Brister, Lari Ann, 142
Bryan, Hannah, Pastor, 64
Bryant, Kenny, 12–13, 15, 17, 123, 148
buffalo horn spoon, 152
Bureau of Indian Affairs (BIA), 34, 131–32
Burleson, John, 116–17
Burrage, David, 129, 176
Burrage, Mike, 176, 192
Burrage, Sean, 129, 176
Burris, Tony, 108–9
Burwick, Jason, 114
Byington, Cyrus, 34
Byington, Presley, 10, 78

Caldwell, Eleanor, 12, 59
calling horn, circa 1861, 11
calling horn, circa 1916, 29
careers. See Tribal diversity
Carney, Alvie N., 108
Carney, Laura, 178
casinos, Choctaw Casino Resort Hotel, 188–89
cattle ranchers, 190–91
caves, Nanih Waiya Cave, 20, 21
Cavin, Dylan, 82
Certificate of Degree in Indian Blood (CDIB), 131–32
Charleston, Choc, 159
Charleston, Steven, Bishop, 65
Cherry, Al, 114
Chicasaw people, 21, 26
child development centers, 162
Choate, Lyman, 91
Choctaw Capitol Building, 108
Choctaw Casino Resort Hotel, 188–89
Choctaw Civil War of 1747–1750, 26
Choctaw Community Centers, 97, 127, 147, 175, 183
Choctaw dolls, 21–22, 25, 26, 167
Choctaw language, 29, 31, 38, 46, 57, 165
Choctaw Nation Color Guard, 116–21
ChoctawNation.com website, 70, 75
Choctaw Nation Historic Preservation Department, 11

Choctaw Nation Princesses, 41, 70–71, 74
Choctaw Nation Tribal Council, 12–13, 15
Choctaw Natural Resources Committee, 194–95
Choctaw University, 164
Christian, Mike, 169
chukka (wooden living structure), 154–55
church. See faith and religion
Clampet, Clara Isabel, 183
clay bowl, 20
Clay, Lacy, 113
Clay, Luke, 113
Clay, Olivia, 113
Coal Creek Cumberland Presbyterian Church, 60–61
Code Talkers, 101, 103, 104–5, 112–13
Coleman, Bill, 13, 124
Coleman, Louis, 11
Coleman, Priscilla, 139
Coley, Joe, 10–11, 12–13, 15, 146
community outreach, 139, 142, 185
Copeland, Larissa, 142
corn, 22, 144
Council, Howard, 157
Cowen, Chester, 81
Cox, Delton, 12–13, 15, 16, 52, 55, 110–11
Cox, Isabelle, 49
creation legends, 20–21
Creek people, 26
Creek War of 1813, 26
Crosby, Ida, 180
Crowley, Sue, 140–41
Culbreath, Joy, 165
cultural heritage: basketry, 41–45, 48–49, 90, 149–52; Choctaw language, 38; pottery classes, 50–51; revitalization of, 28–29; Skullyville Cemetery, 11, 52–55; stickball exhibitions, 47; storytelling, 39–40, 46; Tribal festival at NMAI, 30–31, 36–37; Wheelock Academy, 32–34. See also art and culture
Cultural Services Department, 15
Curnutt, Adrianna, 70–71

dances: Choctaw dancers at NMAI and Capitol grounds, 30–31; social dances, 8–9, 29, 66
Dancing Rabbit Creek Treaty of 1830, 18, 19, 23, 34
Dawes Commission rolls, 13, 128–33
DeHerrera, Sarah, 16
Denny, Ladora, 185
design symbolism, 70
De Soto, Hernando, 25

Dillard, Anthony, 12–13, 15, 110–11, 140–41
Dillard, Janie, 189
Dillard, Misty, 189
disease and European contact, 25
dolls, 21–22, 25, 26, 167
Dosh, Ted, 12–13, 15, 162
Durant Fire Department, 187

Easley, Joseph Den Pah-She-Ka, 60
education: basketry, 48–49; Choctaw language, 29, 31, 38, 46, 57, 165; Choctaw University, 164; Goodland Indian School, 166–67; pottery classes, 50–51; Tribal leaders, 160, 162–67; Wheelock Academy, 11, 32–34
eggs, wild onions and eggs, 146, 149
elbow-shaped basket, 149
elders, 133, 178–81, 183
Espinoza, Virginia, Reverend, 12, 57
European contact, 25–27

faith and religion: Christianity, 56–57, 59; and church meetings, 59–60, 63, 65; Coal Creek Cumberland Presbyterian Church, 60–61; David Wilson, 67; Gene Wilson, 66; Johnson Family Singers, 58; religious conversion, 27, 56–57; Round Lake Cumberland Presbyterian Church, 64; St. Paul's Cathedral, 65; Wheelock Church, 62–63
Family Investment Center, 185
Fassino, Leigh Ann, 139
flutes, 78, 80, 99
Folsom, Kenslee, 50
Folsom, R. D., 182
Folsom, Sue, 40, 73
food: banaha, 151–53; crops and gardening, 145–47; grinding corn, 144; hog fry, 148; rabbit gumbo, 150; traditional food, 153–55; traditional recipes, 149
Fourche Maline Creek, 146
Frazier, James, 12–13, 15, 110–11, 127
Frazier, Tobias, 113
French traders, 26
fry bread, 145, 153
Fry, Marion, 131

Gardner, Stephanie, 163
Gibson, Audie, 116–17
Gilmore, Josephine, 50
Gipson, Nehemiah, 140–41
"Give Me Christ, or Else I Die", 68

Goodland Indian School, 166–67
gourd art, 94
government. See Tribal services and systems
grape dumplings, 149, 153
Great Seal of the Choctaw Nation, 12–13
Green, Kay, 184
Green, Regina, 43
Gwin, Tammy, 189

Hacker, Paul, 80
Halcomb, Denny, 112
Halcomb, Michael, 112
Halcomb, Royce, 112
Hammons, Randy, 139
Hampton, Ben, 112
Hampton, Brenda, 13, 128, 132
Haynes, Jack, 97
healthcare and wellness, 136–39
Heard, Irene Hudson, 181
Heard, Suzanne, 41, 181
helping tradition, 69
Heritage Monday, 29
Hicks, Jack, 190–91
historic preservation, 132
Historic Preservation Department, 15
history: ancestral Choctaw communities, 21–25; creation legends, 20–21; and European contact, 25–27; indigenous Choctaw history, 18–27; oral history, 19, 21–22; revitalizing Choctaw heritage, 28–29. See also cultural heritage
Hobbs, John, 125
hog fry, 148
Holden, Robert, 175
Holy Rosary Catholic Indian Mission Church, 56
homeland, original Choctaw homelands, 20–21
Hooser, Ernest, 156
Hooser, John A., 156
Horst, Tracy, 40
Howe, LeAnne, 84
Howell, Richard, 139
Hudson, Adeline, 144
Hudson, Peter, 181
Hugo Wellness Center, 137
Hunter, Nellie, 116–17, 119
Huser, Yvonne Lyons, 86

Ice Age and ancestral Choctaw communities, 21–25
iksa (moiety) system, 21
Indian Territory, 105, 108
Irish Famine aid, 69
iskvli, 52
"iti naki", 75

Jackson, John, 194–95
Jackson, Kanda, 48
Jackson, Kay, 40

INDEX

Jackson, Teresa, 138
James, Harry, 95
Jefferson, Juanita, 130
Jefferson, Teresa, 87
Jefferson, V. W. "Buster", 175
Jessie, Herbert, 116–17, 121
jewelry, 96
Joe, Brad, 47
John, Aiden Kanalli, 60
John, Loa Mae, 60
Johnson, Bubba, 58
Johnson, Moses, 58
Joines, Roger, 187
Jones Academy, 164, 165
judges, 129, 130–31

Ketchashawno, Betty, 151
Ketchashawno, Cedric, 151
Kiamichi River, 194–95
Kidwell, Clara Sue, 93
Kirkes, Jimmy, 193

Ladd, Charise, 147
Lalli, Miranda, 134–35
Lance, John, 114
Lawless, Beth, 113
Leader, Otis, 105
leadership, Choctaw Nation Tribal Council, 12–17
LeFlore, Greenwood, 104
LeFlore Hall, 34
LeFlore home, 35
LeFlore, Thomas (Chief), 34
LeFlore-Weakley, Naomi, 140–41
Leonard, Mitchell, 131
Lester, Gwen Coleman, 76
Lick Skillet Ranch, 190–91
Lighthorsemen, 13, 103–5, 108, 112
Lloyd, Charlene, 140–41
Loman, Terry, 116–17
Ludlow, Bob, 116–17

Mabilla tribe, 25
Mantaghi, Shirley, 116–17, 120
Marshall, Delores, 112
Martin-Price, Bonita, 140–41
McAffrey, Al, 171
McClain, Brian, 192, 194–95
McCoy, Dara, 113
McCoy, Katie, 113
McCurtain, Edmund (Chief), 55
McDaniel, Jo, 163
McDaniel, Shannon, 142, 194–95
McGuire, Kristie, 74
McKaughan, Kelly, 114
McLarry, Quentin, 114
McMillan, Ruth, 101
"Meditation on Death", 68
Messenger, Tony, 12–13, 15, 17, 185
Mihesuah, Devon, 92
Mik o (Chief), 14, 15
Miko Apelvchi (Assistant Chief), 11, 15
military. See soldiers and the military
missionaries, 27, 31
Mississippi Choctaw breastplate, 5
Mobile River, 25
Moffitt, John, 116–17
Moffitt, Summer, 70–71
Moore, Sampson, 116–17
Moore, Sylvester, 125
Morris, Callie, 134–35
"Mother Mound", 21
mounds: construction of, 22; Moundville, 22, 25; Nanih Waiya mound, 19, 20–21
Moundville, 22, 25
Mullin, Mitch, 17, 129
Mushulatubbee (warrior Chief), 12, 13, 70

Nanih Waiya Cave, 20, 21
Nanih Waiya mound, 19, 20–21
National Congress of American Indians (NCAI), 175
National Museum of the American Indian (NMAI), 29, 30, 36–37, 39, 40

Oakes, Brent, 114
O'Brien, Joseph, 116–17
Ogle, Judy, 184
Oklahoma, and Choctaw Trail of Tears, 11, 19, 27
Oklahombi, Joseph, 104
onions, wild onions and eggs, 146, 149
oral history, 19, 21–22
"oski naki", 75
Ouellette, Rachel, 167

Panki Bok Cumberland Presbyterian Church, 60
Parker, Steven, 131
pashova, 151
Pate, Bob, 12–13, 15, 17, 110–11, 134–35
Pate, Jack, 190–91
Pearl River, 25
Penz, Jeff, 189
people of the Choctaw Nation. See Tribal diversity
Perkins, Edmon, 77
Perry, Ron, 12–13, 15, 17, 136
Phelps, Pat, 131
pistols, 105
Pitchlynn, Peter (Chief), 105, 123, 182
Pittman, December, 140–41
pottery: bowls, 22, 24; clay bottle, 27; pottery classes, 50–51, 145, 152; traditional Choctaw pottery, 24
pow wows, Presley Byington in full regalia, 10
princesses, Choctaw Nation Princesses, 41, 70–71, 74
Princess Pale Moon, 86
Project Falvmmichi anti-bullying program, 177
Pushmataha (warrior Chief), 12, 13, 70, 109, 122
Pushmataha Hall, 32
Pyle, Gregory E. (Chief), 14, 15, 16, 17, 23, 106–7, 113, 122, 143, 194–95
Pyle, Patti, 17

quilting, 179

rabbit gumbo, 150
Rabon, Bob, 192
recycling, 143
Reed, Lisa, 40, 142
regalia, Presley Byington in full regalia, 10
religion. See faith and religion
removal and Trail of Tears, 11, 19, 27, 28–29, 31, 33
Renegar, Theresa, 96
Richard, Claire, 177
Roach, Kelsie, 134–35
Roberts, Dustin, 170
Roberts, Lillie, 38
Robison, Benny, 142
Rodgers, Greg, 40
Round Lake Cumberland Presbyterian Church, 64
Rowland, Angel, 194–95
Rowland, Rainette Womack, 187

Sardis Lake, 193
Scholarship Advisement Program (SAP), 162–63
Scott, Jimmie, 60
Scott, Lena, 58
Scott, Linda, 60
Scott, Nathan, Reverend, 60–61
Scott, Seneca, 173
Scroggins, Terri, Captain, 106–7
Self, Georgia Mae, 133
servant leadership, 14–17
Sewell, Chris, 96
Sexton, Isaac, 186
Sharp, Sarah "Beloved", 155
shoulder sash, 4
shoulder sash with bell, 11
Shults, Vonna, 40, 150
silversmithing, 95
singing: Choctaw hymns, 57, 68; and church meetings, 65; Johnson Family Singers, 58
Sisco, Leroy, Lt. General (Ret.), 106–7
Skullyville Cemetery, 11, 52–55
Sleeper, Lana, 40
Smalling, D. G., 79
smoking pipe hatchet, 12
social dances, 8–9, 29, 66
soldiers and the military: Choctaw Defense manufacturing, 115; Choctaw Nation Color Guard, 116–21; Code Talkers, 101, 103, 104–5, 112–13; Korean War, 109; Lighthorsemen, 13, 103–5, 108, 112; Lt. Col. Bobby Yandell, 100; Major General Rita Aragon (Ret.), 102; pilots, 114; Pushmataha (warrior Chief), 109–11, 122; Veteran's Advocacy Program, 114; World War II veterans, 106–7, 108
Southerland-Holmes, Nancy, 88
sovereignty and pre-European contact, 25
Spalding, Florence, 183
Spanish soldiers, 25–26
Spears, Brad, 164
Stallard, Athena, 50
Standefer, Chantelle, 113
Steele, Eveline, 44
Stevens, Emily, 51
Stevens, Phillip, 49
Stewart, Cal, 190–91
stickball blanket, 88
stickball cap, 46
stickball exhibitions, 47
stickball sets, 13, 181
Stigler Health Clinic, 136
storytelling, 39, 40, 46, 63, 65
St. Paul's Cathedral, 65
Sturch, Kathy, 85
symbolism of designs, 70

tanchi labona, 149, 153
Taylor, Neal, 24
Teague, Clayton, 134–35
Teague, Sheldon, 134–35
Tehauno, Amber Nicole, 70–71
Thompson, Amy, 24
Thompson, Dr. Ian, 11, 24
Thompson, Perry, 12–13, 15, 17, 110–11, 137
Timberman, Gena, 161
Tingle, Tim, 16, 39, 99
Todd, Verna, 98
Tombigbee River, 22, 25
Tom, Melvin, 116–17
Trail of Tears, 11, 19, 27, 28–29, 31, 33
treaties: Dancing Rabbit Creek Treaty of 1830, 18, 19, 23, 34; and land cession, 27; Treaty of Fort Adams, 26; Treaty of Hopewell, 26
Tribal Councils, 134–35, 140–41, 142
Tribal diversity: attorneys, 176, 192; buffalo ranching, 193; casinos, 188–89; cattle ranchers, 190–91; Choctaw Constitution Committee, 158; Choctaw Natural Resources Committee, 194–95; community center leader, 175; community outreach, 185; educators, 160, 162–67; elders, 133, 178–81, 183; election board, 184; firefighters, 187; legislative advocacy, 192; museum director, 161; NCAI deputy director, 175; newspaper reporter, 174; photographers, 187; policemen, 186; Project Falvmmichi anti-bullying program, 177; saddle making, 157; state government representatives, 168–73, 176; trading posts, 159; Tribal Councils, 193; Tuskahoma Female Institute, 156, 181; university professor, 160
Tribal services and systems: BISKINIK newspaper, 15, 75, 142; Brenda Hampton, 128; Choctaw Community Centers, 97, 127, 147, 175, 183; community outreach, 139, 142, 185; and Dawes Commission rolls, 128–33; healthcare and wellness, 136–39; historic preservation, 132; judges, 129, 130–31; recycling, 143; Tribal Chaplain Bertram Bobb, 126; Tribal Councils, 134–35, 140–41, 142
Tuscaloosa (Chief), 25
Tuskahoma Female Institute, 156, 181
Tvshka Homma, 29, 43, 193

Umsted, Jane Semple, 83
United Methodist Church, Oklahoma City University, 67
United States Freedom Award, 15

Veteran's Advocacy Program, 114
Vietta, John, 187

Walker, Tandy, 55
Walley, Willie, 147
warrior pride. See soldiers and the military
Watkins, Joe, 160
Watson, Betty, 181
Watson, Frank, 158
Wesley, John, 114
West, Bob, 174
Westbrook, Shelly, 94
Wheelock Academy, 11, 32–34
Wheelock Church, 62–63
whiskey peddlers, 104, 108
whistles, 34
White, Kim, 142
wild onions and eggs, 146, 149
Wilkerson, Cherish, 134–35
Wilkerson, DaNetta, 134–35
Williams, Olin, 46
Williams, Shauna, 163
Williams, Twauna, 163
Williston, Les, 155
Williston, Thomas, 12–13, 15, 17, 62–63, 110–11
Willmott, Rhonda, 116–17, 118
Wilson, David, 67
Wilson, Gene, 66
Winship, Oneida, 185
wood sculptures and carving, 91, 97
Work, P. K., 89
Wright, Alfred, Reverend, 33, 34
Wylie, Wayne, 194–95

Yandell, Bobby, Lt. Col., 100
Youth Empowerment Program, 177